COMPLETE EDITION

BLUES KEYBOARD

MW00848741

Approved Curriculum

Beginning • Intermediate • Mastering

TRICIA WOODS
MERRILL CLARK

Alfred, the leader in educational music publishing, and the National Keyboard Workshop, one of America's finest keyboard schools, have joined forces to bring you the best, most progressive educational tools possible. We hope you will enjoy this book and encourage you to look for other fine products from Alfred and the National Keyboard Workshop.

CONTENTS

Alfred Music Publishing Co., Inc.
P.O. Box 10003
Van Nuys, CA 91410-0003
alfred.com

ISBN-10: 0-7390-7891-7 (Book & CD)
ISBN-13: 978-0-7390-7891-4 (Book & CD)

Cover photograph by Karen Miller.

Blues Keyboard: Complete Edition is dedicated to the memory of Tricia Woods (1966–2011).

 Alfred Cares. Contents printed on 100% recycled paper.

BEGINNING BLUES KEYBOARD

TRICIA WOODS

*This book was acquired, edited, and produced
by Workshop Arts, Inc., the publishing arm of
the National Keyboard Workshop.*

Nathaniel Gunod, editor
Joe Bouchard, music typesetter
Cathy Bolduc, interior design
Audio tracks recorded at Bar None Studio, Cheshire, CT

ABOUT THE AUTHOR

PHOTO • JEREMY MOSS/COURTESY OF TRISHA WOODS

Tricia Woods grew up practicing the piano in the basement of her family's Tupper Lake, New York home. Her first professional music experiences were as a teenager, playing church organ in the Adirondacks. Tricia earned a degree in biology from Brown University before resuming her musical studies at the University of Washington and Cornish College of the Arts in Seattle, WA. While in the Northwest, she led several original music groups, was featured at Seattle's Bumbershoot Festival and studied at the Banff International Jazz Workshop. Tricia moved to New York City in 1995 and resides in Brooklyn. In addition to leading her group, "Les Fauves," an original seven-piece brass and rhythm section ensemble, she performs on piano, keyboards and sings in a number of styles including blues, jazz and soul. She has played numerous venues in and around the New York area including The Knitting Factory, Manny's Car Wash and Smalls. Tricia teaches keyboards at the National Keyboard Workshop in New Milford, CT.

CONTENTS

Track 1

An MP3 CD is included with this book to make learning easier and more enjoyable. The symbol shown at bottom left appears next to every example in the book that features an MP3 track. Use the MP3s to ensure you're capturing the feel of the examples and interpreting the rhythms correctly. The track number below the symbol corresponds directly to the example you want to hear (example numbers are above the icon). All the track numbers are unique to each "book" within this volume, meaning every book has its own Track 1, Track 2, and so on. (For example, *Beginning Blues Keyboard* starts with Track 1, as does *Intermediate Blues Keyboard* and *Mastering Blues Keyboard*.) Track 1 will help you tune an electronic keyboard to this CD.

The disc is playable on any CD player equipped to play MP3 CDs. To access the MP3s on your computer, place the CD in your CD-ROM drive. In Windows, double-click on My Computer, then right-click on the CD icon labeled "MP3 Files" and select Explore to view the files and copy them to your hard drive. For Mac, double-click on the CD icon on your desktop labeled "MP3 Files" to view the files and copy them to your hard drive.

INTRODUCTION

Welcome to *The Complete Blues Keyboard Method,* a comprehensive series of books designed specifically for the aspiring blues keyboardist. This method consists of three separate volumes now available in this complete edition. Each of the three volumes (*Beginning Blues Keyboard, Intermediate Blues Keyboard* and *Mastering Blues Keyboard*) is an important step along the way to mastering the blues on the keyboard.

The first part, *Beginning Blues Keyboards,* is about understanding the blues and putting the blues on the keyboard. The *Intermediate* and *Mastering* sections, which follow, build upon the concepts introduced here, taking a closer look at specific blues styles and more advanced playing techniques.

To play blues keyboard you must ask yourself, "What is the Blues?" It's a loaded question. It evokes different answers from different people—whether they're playing, listening to or living the blues. In my opinion, anyone can learn to play the blues. Anyone who really wants to play the blues, however, will listen to the music and the stories of the men and women who have played the blues before us, and will investigate the history of this music. It will become clear then that playing the blues is about more than just chords and melodies and rhythms. It will become clear that finding a way to express the *spirit* of the blues through your playing is what it's all about.

Maybe you come to this book already loving and listening to the blues. In that case, it is my hope that these lessons will help you start putting the sounds you already love onto a keyboard. Even if you are a total beginner, you will be playing the blues in a surprisingly short amount of time. If you aren't very familiar with the blues, I hope this book serves as your introduction to an incredibly alluring and inspiring world of music. You might be surprised to know how much the blues is around you already, just because you are here now. Most modern popular music in our culture that was not influenced by the blues. Rock'n'roll came straight out of the blues. Jazz absorbed the blues. Funk and soul music came from the blues. *To play any of these musical styles, you need to play the blues.*

And the best part of playing the blues is that it can be as simple or as involved as you want it to be. You can learn to play a blues progression quite easily. You can also spend a lifetime learning to be a great blues player. On the keyboard, there are a million ways to play the blues. We won't get to all of them in this book. We will, however, cover the basics and take a look at different styles, including Chicago blues and boogie-woogie. We'll talk about playing in a band. When you reach the end of the book, you'll have a lot of the tools and vocabulary you need to speak the language of the blues on the keyboard. Then all you need to do is keep listening, keep playing and keep living the blues.

ACKNOWLEDGMENTS

Many thanks to Nat Gunod and Joe Bouchard at Workshop Arts, to Alfred Music Publishing and the National Guitar/Keyboard Workshop for making this project possible. Thanks to Murali Coryell, Bill Foster and Russ Meissner for your musicianship, inspiration, guidance and friendship. Thanks also to: Peter Karl at Fifth House Studios; Marshall Chess, Bill Greensmith, John Rockwood, Bill Weilbacker, the National Blues Archive and the Rutgers Institute of Jazz Studies for help in acquiring photos; to Bruce Katz, Brian Mitchell, Dan Cazio and Merrill Clarck for sharing expertise; to Heather, Lois, Caroline, Briggan, Arnold, Andrew and Gregory for bending ears and lending patience and support; to my piano teachers, Joanne Brackeen, Randy Halberstadt, Dave Peck and especially Jerome Gray and Marc Seales who taught me to play the blues first; and to my family for unwittingly bestowing on me the gift of a life in music. This project is dedicated to all of the men and women who have played the blues and have given us this incredible musical heritage.

CHAPTER 1

Music Review

The goal of the *Beginning* section of this book is to get you playing blues piano, even if you don't know anything about it yet. It does assume that you have a little experience at the piano, and it will require you to read music. This chapter reviews some basic music and keyboard concepts to get you started.

THE GRAND STAFF, CLEFS AND LEDGER LINES

Piano music contains notes written in both the *treble clef* and the *bass clef*. Generally, the notes in the treble clef are played with the right hand, and the notes in the bass clef are played with the left hand.

 Sign for the bass or "F" clef
The two dots surround the line for the note F.

 Sign for the treble or "G" clef
The curled part surrounds the line for the note G.

The treble and bass clefs together make up the *grand staff*.

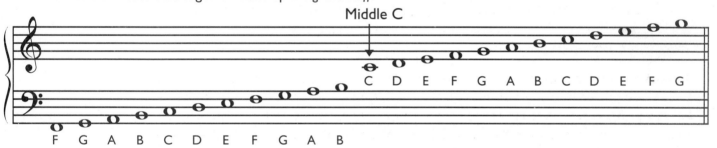

Middle C is in the middle of the grand staff. It sits on a *ledger line* because it lies between the two clefs and is an extension of either one. Ledger lines function exactly like lines in the staff. We can further extend either the treble or the bass clef by as many ledger lines as necessary above or below the staff.

Ledger lines in the treble clef.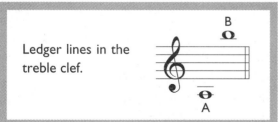

Ledger lines in the bass clef.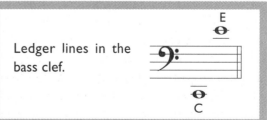

It is important to become very familiar with where notes lie on the keyboard.

Middle
C

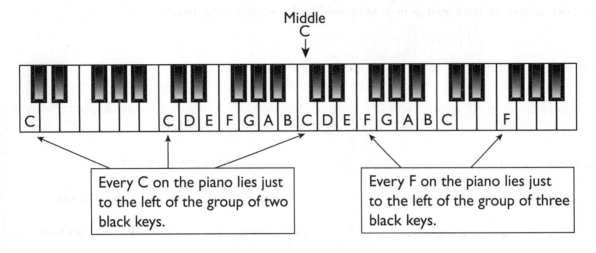

Every C on the piano lies just to the left of the group of two black keys.

Every F on the piano lies just to the left of the group of three black keys.

HALF STEPS AND ACCIDENTALS

An *interval* is the distance between any two pitches. The smallest interval between two pitches is a *half step*. On the piano, any key is a half step away from the key closest to it on either its left or right side.

Half   Half
Step   Step

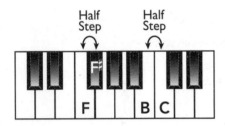

On the piano, a half step may fall between either a white key and a black key, or in some cases, two white keys. There are two places on the keyboard where two white notes are a half step apart: between E and F and between B and C.

Notes written with a sharp sign ♯ or a flat sign ♭ before them are called *accidentals*.

A *sharp sign* ♯ raises the *pitch* (degree of highness or lowness) of a note a half step. Play the key which, on the keyboard, lies directly to the right of the written note.

A *flat sign* ♭ lowers the pitch of a note a half step. Play the key lying directly to the left of the written note.

Accidentals remain in force for the duration on the measure they are in unless cancelled by a natural sign ♮.

The black key to the right of C is C♯. The same key is also D♭!

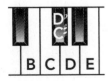

C♯ and D♭ are *enharmonic equivalents*—two notes which indicate the same pitch—but have different names. Which name a note is given depends upon how that note functions in a particular melody or chord. We'll see examples of this when we discuss scales and keys.

RHYTHMIC VALUES OF NOTES, RESTS AND MEASURES

One of the most important elements of the blues is *rhythm* (the organization of music in time using long and short note values). Feeling the beat, or pulse behind the music, and having control over where in time you play a note, will make your playing much more convincing.

Rhythmic notation is used in written music to assign time values to the notes and rests on the page.

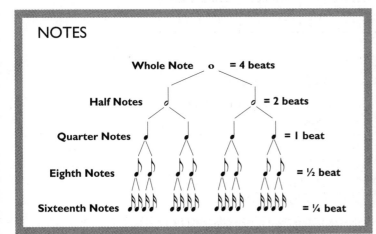

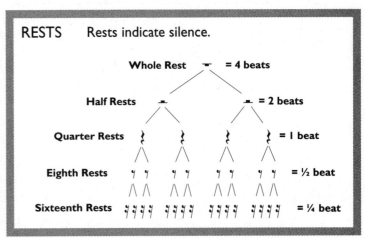

When counting notes or rests that get less than one beat, we need to subdivide the beat.

> Count eighth notes or rests as "one-and, two-and…" etc.
> Count sixteenth notes and rests as "one-e-and-a, two-e-and-a…" etc.

DOTS
A dot following a note or rest increases the duration of the note or rest by one half:

> two beats + one beat = 3 beats ——————————
> one beat + half a beat = one and one half beats ————

TIES
Two notes tied together means hold the note through the duration of the sum of both notes.

> two beats + one beat = three beats ——————————

TIME SIGNATURES AND MEASURES

Music is divided into *measures* (also called *bars*) which are indicated in written music with vertical lines on the staff called *bar lines*. Each measure contains a particular number of beats. In the blues, as in most popular music, it is usual for each measure to contain four beats, and sometimes three beats.

The *time signature* appears just after the key signature of a tune and contains two numbers showing how many beats each measure contains, and what kind of note gets one beat.

$\frac{4}{4}$ ——The top number indicates four beats per measure.
——The bottom number means that the quarter note ♩ gets one beat.

𝄴 is a symbol which means *common time*, which is another way of saying $\frac{4}{4}$ (the most commonly-encountered time signature).

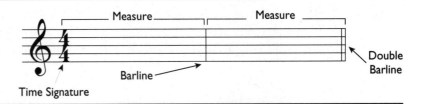

The major scale is made up of seven notes which, when played in sequence, make the familiar melody: do, re, mi, fa, sol, la, ti, (do). The scale is constructed by starting on any note and following this pattern of whole step and half step intervals:

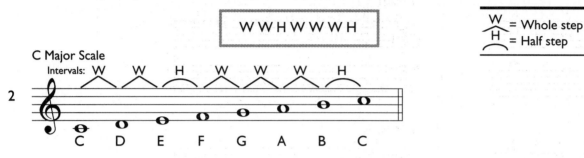

W W H W W W H

W ‿ = Whole step
H ‿ = Half step

C Major Scale
Intervals: W W H W W W H

2

C D E F G A B C

In order to keep the pattern, each scale has its own combination of flats or sharps. On the piano, this means each major scale has a different arrangement of black and white notes.

D Major Scale
Intervals: W W H W W W H

3

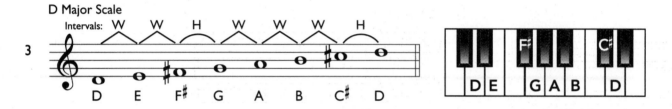

D E F# G A B C# D

The *key signature* contains the flats or sharps specific to a major scale. The name of the key is the same as the note the scale started from, which we call the *root*.

Here are the key signatures for all the major keys:

FINGERINGS FOR MAJOR SCALES

The *fingering* (order of the fingers used) for each scale depends on its pattern of white and black notes. There is an easiest way to play each major scale on the piano. Here they are:

Practice Tip:

A good way to learn and practice your scales is to divide each one into two groups. Each scale will have one group of three fingers and one group of four fingers. Play all the notes of each group as a *cluster* (all together) up and down the keyboard. Your hand will quickly become familiar with the feel of that particular scale.

INTERVALS

All of the different intervals we use in music have numeric names. For instance, another name for a half step is a *minor second*. This may also be called a *flat second* and written as ♭2.

Two half steps together equal one *whole step*, also called a major second, and written as 2.

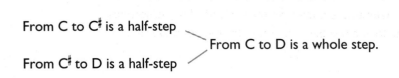

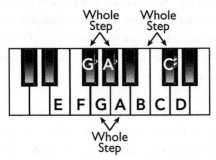

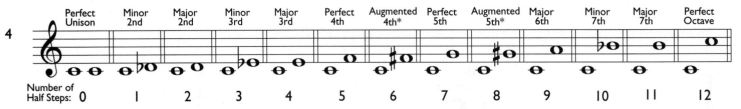

There are twelve half steps in an *octave*. An octave is the closest distance between any two notes with the same name.

THE INTERVALS IN AN OCTAVE

Number	Number of Half Steps	Interval	Abbreviation
1	0	perfect unison	PU
♭2	1	minor 2nd	min2
2	2	major 2nd	Maj2
♭3	3	minor 3rd	min3
3	4	major 3rd	Maj3
4	5	perfect 4th	P4
♯4 ∗	6 ("tritone")	augmented 4th	Aug4
♭5 ∗	6 ("tritone")	diminished 5th	dim5
5	7	perfect 5th	P5
♯5 ∗	8	augmented 5th	Aug5
♭6 ∗	8	minor 6th	min6
6	9	major 6th	Maj6
♭7	10	minor 7th	min7
7	11	major 7th	Maj7
1	12	perfect octave	P8

∗If the F♯ in the augmented 4th is respelled as G♭, the interval is called a diminished 5th. If the G♯ in the augmented 5th is respelled as A♭, the interval is called a minor 6th. The augmented 4th and diminished 5th intervals are enharmonically the same and sometimes called a tritone.

INTERVAL INVERSION

Intervals in music are often inverted. The total number of half steps in any interval plus its inversion add up to one octave (twelve half steps).

For example: The inversion of a major 3rd (four half steps) = a minor 6th (eight half steps). 8 + 4 = 12.

> *Exercise:*
> Check your understanding of intervals: starting from a note other than C, see if you can name all the intervals one-by-one and find each interval on the keyboard.

Notice that the major scales on page 11 moved from key to key at an interval of a perfect 5th each time a sharp or flat was added to the key signature. For the sharp keys, we moved up in 5ths. For flat keys, we moved down in 5ths. In addition, each new sharp note added to the key signature was a perfect 5th above the last one, and each new flat note added was a perfect 5th below the last one. This movement is known as the *cycle of 5ths* (sometimes called the *circle* of 5ths). The cycle of 5ths forms the basis for most harmonic movement in popular music.

Since an inverted perfect 5th is a perfect 4th, part of the cycle of 5ths is sometimes called the cycle of 4ths. It's the same thing. Usually, when blues players think "cycle of 5ths," they are thinking counter-clockwise through the cycle—down by 5ths: C, F, B♭, E♭, etc.

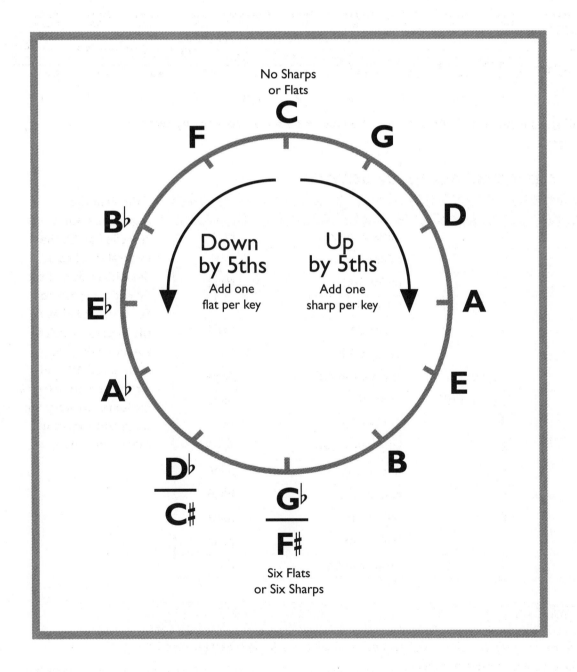

Let's look at what happens if we play all the notes found in the C Major scale, starting on the note A. The scale now has a very different sound because it has become a minor scale—A Minor. The key signature for A Minor is the same as the key signature for C Major. There are no sharps or flats in it. For each major key, there is a *relative minor key* which shares the same key signature.

The relative minor key's root is the 6th degree of the major scale.

For example, in the key of C Major, the 6th degree of the scale is A:

C	D	E	F	G	A	B
1	2	3	4	5	6	7

So, the relative minor to C Major is A Minor and the scale, called the *natural minor scale,* contains the same notes, but starting in a different place in the order:

A	B	C	D	E	F	G
1	2	3	4	5	6	7

The pattern of half steps and whole steps for the natural minor scale is:

W	H	W	W	H	W	W

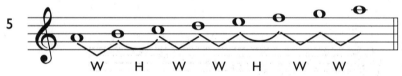

Look at the cycle of 5ths again. The major key cycle is on the inside. The relative minor for each major key is outside the circle. Just like the major keys, the minor keys move up in 5ths as you add sharps, and down in 5ths as you add flats to the key signature.

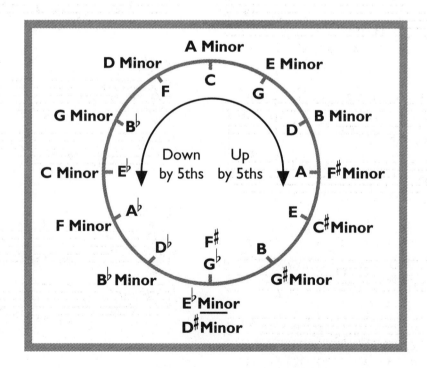

FINGERINGS FOR NATURAL MINOR SCALES

The chart below shows the notes and best fingerings for the twelve natural minor scales.

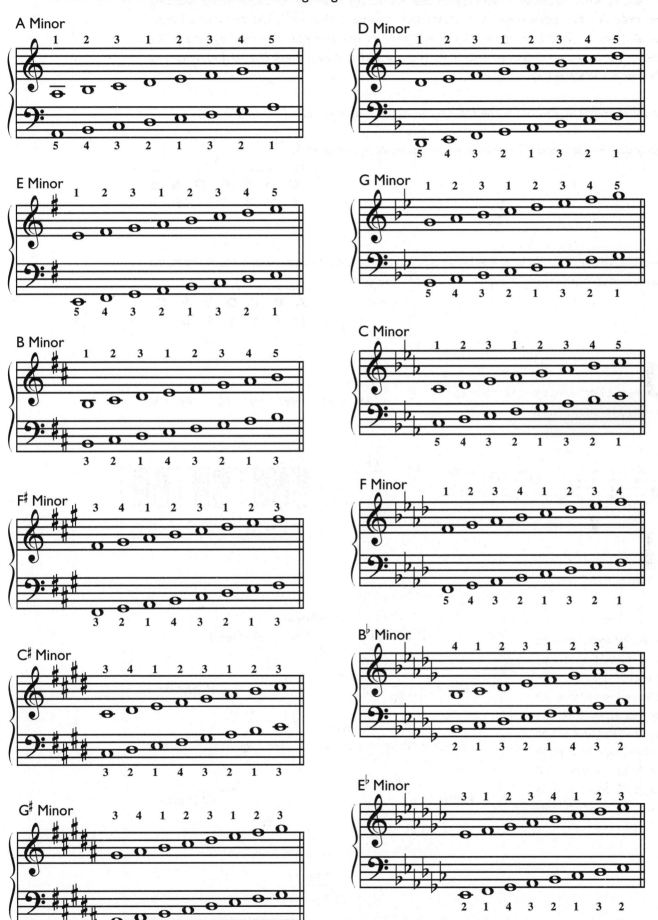

The first *chords* (three or more notes played simultaneously) we'll use to play the blues, are three-note chords called *triads*. Triads are made by putting two 3rd intervals (major 3rds or minor 3rds) on top of each other.

You can build a major triad by taking the root (1), 3rd (3) and 5th (5) of the major scale:

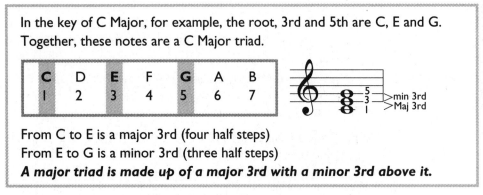

In the key of C Major, for example, the root, 3rd and 5th are C, E and G. Together, these notes are a C Major triad.

From C to E is a major 3rd (four half steps)
From E to G is a minor 3rd (three half steps)
A major triad is made up of a major 3rd with a minor 3rd above it.

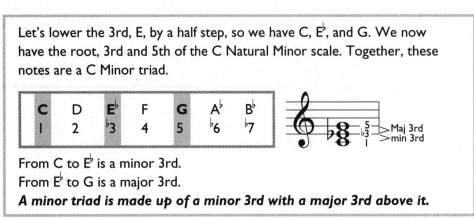

Let's lower the 3rd, E, by a half step, so we have C, E♭, and G. We now have the root, 3rd and 5th of the C Natural Minor scale. Together, these notes are a C Minor triad.

From C to E♭ is a minor 3rd.
From E♭ to G is a major 3rd.
A minor triad is made up of a minor 3rd with a major 3rd above it.

There are two other types of triads which we will encounter less frequently.

Diminished triad — A minor triad with a lowered 5th. For example: C, E♭, G♭.   Abbreviation: C° or Cdim.
Augmented triad — A major triad with a raised 5th. For example: C, E, G♯.   Abbreviation: CAug

Here is an exercise for learning major and minor triads in twelve keys, going through the cycle of 5ths.

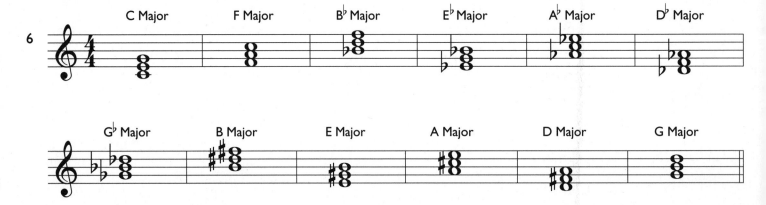

When you are comfortable with the major triads, play through the exercise again, this time lowering the 3rd of each triad by a half step to make it minor.

DIATONIC TRIADS

Diatonic means "of the key." *Diatonic triads* are triads created from notes found within the scale of a particular key.

Every major scale contains the following pattern of major, minor and diminished triads:

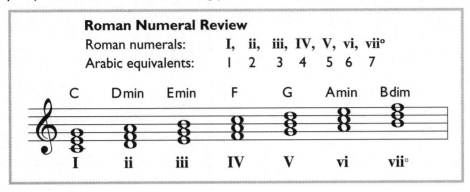

Roman Numeral Review

Roman numerals:	I,	ii,	iii,	IV,	V,	vi,	vii°
Arabic equivalents:	1	2	3	4	5	6	7

We use Roman numerals to label the diatonic triads according to the degree of the scale they are built on. Large numerals indicate major triads. Small numerals indicate minor triads.

Let's take the key of C and build a triad on each degree of the scale using only notes found in the C Major scale.

C D E F G A B C

From the root the notes are C, E and G—a C Major triad. This is the I chord.

From the second note of the scale, the notes are D, F and A—a D Minor triad. This is the ii chord.

Continuing up the scale we'll get:

E Minor, iii
F Major, IV
G Major, V
A Minor, vi
B Diminished, vii°

The natural minor scale contains the following pattern of diatonic triads:

i, ii°, III, iv, v, VI, VII

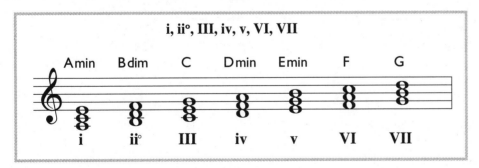

For example, in the key of C Minor (C D E♭ F G A♭ B♭ C), the diatonic triads are:

C	Minor	i
D	Diminished	ii°
E♭	Major	III
F	Minor	iv
G	Minor	v
A♭	Major	VI
B♭	Major	VII

Exercise:

Starting with a G Major triad, play all the diatonic triads in the key of G. Notice whether each triad you play is major, minor or diminished. Did you get the correct pattern of triads for a major key?

Measures are the building blocks of songs. The time signature, the number of measures in a song and the harmonic pattern (sequence of chords) through the measures constitutes a song's form.

In popular music, songs are often written as *lead sheets*. In a lead sheet, the melody is written, but the harmony is indicated only by chord symbols over the measures.

Let's look at the following "mini-song" and describe its form:

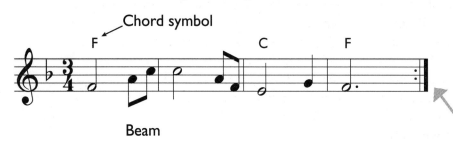

Chord symbol

Beam

Notice that when eighth notes are written consecutively, they are beamed together.

A double bar with two dots is a *repeat sign*. This sign indicates that the example should be repeated.

The key signature is F Major. The time signature is $\frac{3}{4}$. This means there are three beats per bar, and the quarter note gets one beat. The form is four bars long. The harmonic movement is from the I chord (F) to the V chord (C) and back. The repeat sign indicates that the form is played twice.

Here are some of the various symbols used in lead sheets for the basic triads.

Chord	Possible Symbols	Formula
C Major	C, CMaj, CM, C△	1, 3, 5
C minor	Cmin, Cmi, Cm, C-	1, ♭3, 5
C Augmented	CAug, C+	1, 3, ♯5
C diminished	Cdim, C°	1, ♭3, ♭5

TEMPO INDICATIONS

In this book, the tempo (speed) of the music is indicated with *metronome markings*. A metronome is a device that produces a clicking sound at a specific rate of speed measured in beats per minute. For instance, a tempo of one beat per second, or sixty beats per minute, in a time signature where the quarter note equals one beat, will look like this:

♩ = 60

Now, let's continue and play the blues...

CHAPTER 2

The Twelve-Bar Blues

If you ask someone who loves the blues what the blues means to them, they are unlikely to start talking about chords. But if you're on the bandstand and the leader calls a "blues in G," then he is talking about chords and a specific form. It's the *twelve-bar blues*. There are a number of different blues forms, but twelve bars is by far the most common. Typically, the twelve bars are divided into three four-bar phrases. The second phrase generally repeats the first, and the third is a response to the first two. This pattern echoes the "call and response" tradition of African music which is at the root of all blues music. In a call and response situation, a leader will "call"

a phrase and the crowd will repeat it. This became standard practice in African American churches. The three-phrase form was adopted by early blues singers who were often improvising lyrics as they sang. The harmonic structure varied somewhat, but over the years a specific chord progression emerged: four bars of I, two bars of IV, two bars of I, one bar of V, one bar of IV and two bars of I. This chord progression has been in use for nearly a century and is so pervasive in both blues and rock music that it is certain not to disappear anytime soon.

The example below outlines the form of a basic twelve-bar blues. The form is twelve bars long. In other words, the harmonic pattern, or chord progression, repeats itself every twelve bars. Each time through the progression is referred to as a *chorus*. When you begin to improvise on blues "changes," this is the chord progression you will be playing over. In this example, you'll be playing the root of the chord in your left hand, and the major triad in your right hand.

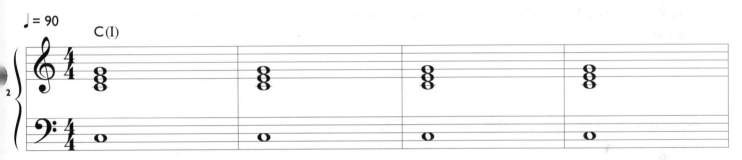

> There are only three chords in the twelve-bar blues progression, and they are all diatonic to the key of the blues. They are the I, the IV and the V chords.

Since we know that every major key has the same pattern of diatonic triads, we can use the Roman numerals from the twelve-bar form on page 19 to figure out the blues progression in another key.

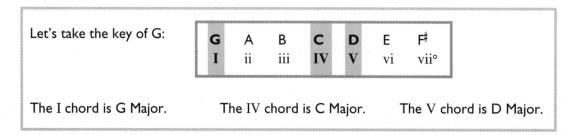

Let's take the key of G:

G	A	B	C	D	E	F#
I	ii	iii	IV	V	vi	vii°

The I chord is G Major.   The IV chord is C Major.   The V chord is D Major.

Here is the twelve-bar blues in the key of G Major. In your left hand, play the root of the chord on the first beat of each measure. In your right hand, play a major triad on each beat of the measure. Memorize this progression.

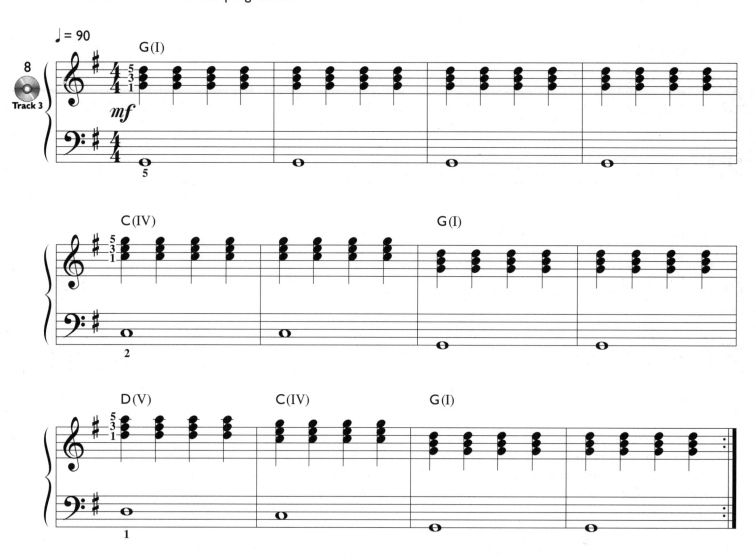

𝑚𝑓 = This is a *dynamic marking*. Dynamic markings represent the various levels of volume. This one, *mezzo forte*, means moderately loud.

Exercise:
Transpose the example above into the key of F. Find the I, IV and V chords in that key. Follow the twelve-bar blues form, playing triads in your right hand and the roots of the chords in your left hand.

We can make melodies using only the notes of the three triads. The next example is a blues in the key of G Major. Each triad is *arpeggiated*. Arpeggiation is playing the notes of a chord one at a time. Notice the dotted-quarter-note rhythm we are playing in the right hand. Later on, we'll put this in the left hand for some New Orleans-style playing. Look below for help in counting this new rhythm.

MARDI GRAS
Track 4

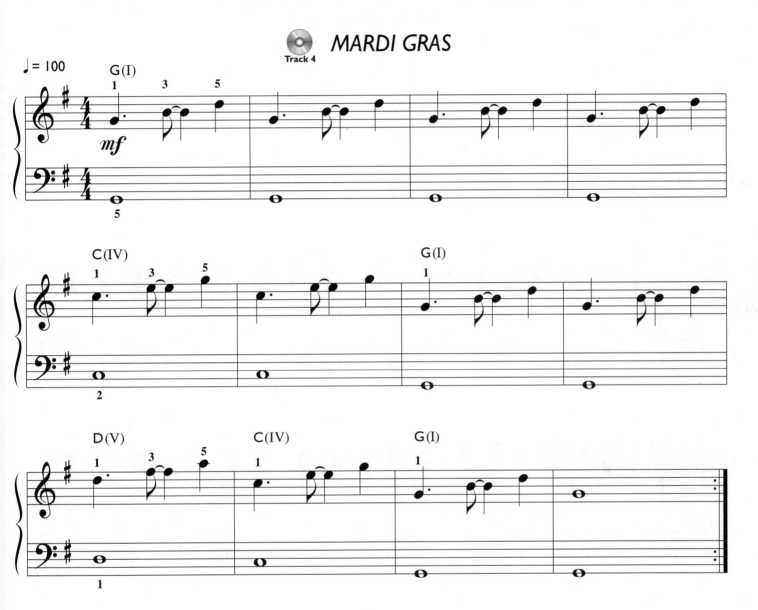

Counting Dotted Quarter Note Rhythms

To count a measure of music accurately, start by finding the note with the smallest rhythmic value. In this case it is the eighth note, which gets half of a beat. Since there are two eighth notes in each beat, we will divide each beat in two and count the four beats of the bar as "one-and-two-and-three-and-four-and."

$$\frac{4}{4} \quad \text{♩.} \quad \text{♪♩} \quad \text{♩}$$

1 (&2) & (3 &) 4 (&)

In this rhythm, the first quarter note is dotted, so the second note played falls on the "and" of two. Since the second note is tied through the third beat, the next note we play falls on beat four.

TRIPLETS

Let's make our twelve-bar blues progression sound more like the blues. This example has a $\frac{12}{8}$ feel. The time signature is still $\frac{4}{4}$, but we're going to take each quarter note and divide it into three. In other words, we'll play *eighth-note triplets*. Instead of playing two eighth notes per beat, you are going to play three. Each bar will then contain twelve triplet eighth-notes, which is why it is called $\frac{12}{8}$ feel, or triplet feel.

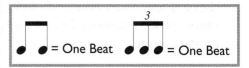

Let's get used to this feel by staying on the I chord, C Major, and playing eighth-note triplets with your right hand. Set your metronome to about 70 beats per minute and play three triplet eighth-notes on each click.

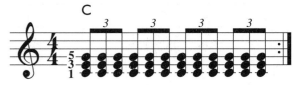

Now play through the blues progression in C Major, playing constant eighth-note triplets in your right hand. Be sure to keep your hand relaxed. Your wrist will get a workout.

TIP:
All the triads are fingered 1,3,5.

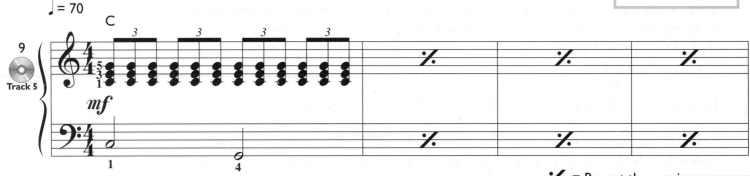

$\dot{\,} = $ Repeat the previous measure.

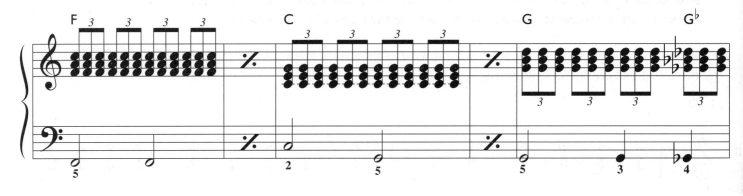

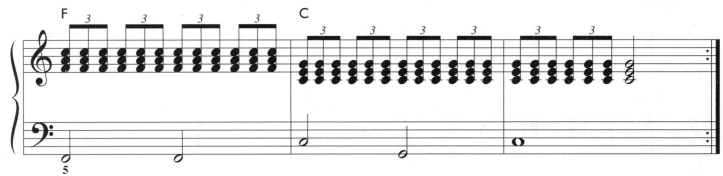

As you play the blues, you will get used to *hearing* all three parts of the triplet in the beat, but you won't always want to *play* on all three parts. Play example 9 again, this time emphasizing the first and third eighth note of each beat, and "ghosting" the second note so that you barely hear it. It's worth your time to get comfortable with this feel. It's an integral part of blues keyboard playing.

INVERTING TRIADS

So far we've been playing all of our triads in root position. In other words, the root of the chord is the lowest note in the chord, the 3rd is next and the 5th is the highest. We have more sounds to choose from if we rearrange the position of the notes in the chords. This is called *inverting* the triads.

Every triad has three positions:

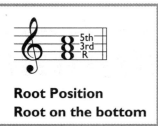

Root Position
Root on the bottom

1st Inversion
3rd on the bottom

R = Root

2nd Inversion
5th on the bottom

Inversions are used to create good *voice leading* in a chord progression The goal of good voice leading is to create smooth melodic movements in the different voices. Each note of a chord can be thought of as a voice in a choir. As we move from chord to chord, each voice moves to its next note. For instance, all the top notes in the chords comprise the highest voice. As the harmonies you play get more complex, it will become more and more important to pay attention to voice leading.

Let's look at a twelve-bar blues in F Major to see how we might use inversions.

The I chord sounds strong with the root as its top note, so we'll start with F Major in first inversion. We can then play the B♭ chord (IV) in root position without having to move our hand very much. This creates a smoother sound at the chord change, especially since the top note of the chord doesn't change. For the C chord, we'll play another root position triad because it's just a whole step away, and then back to the F chord in 1st inversion.

In this example, play the triads with your right hand and with your left hand, play the root of the chord on beat one of each measure.

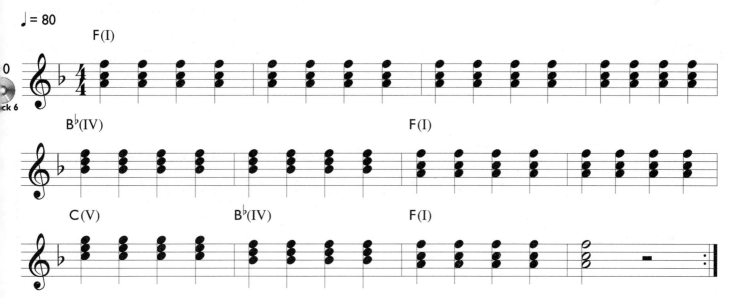

Notice that the left hand part is not written out in the music. This is common in blues, jazz and pop music. If you use any music at all, it is likely to be a *lead sheet*, with melody and chord names only. The rest is up to you. In this case it's easy. You know from the name of the chord, which is the name of the root note. Play root whole notes in the left hand.

If you're going to play the blues in different keys and use inversions that sound good, you need to have all of the triads right under your fingers. Let's look at some exercises to learn triads.

1. Play root position triads down through the cycle of 5ths, holding each chord for four beats. Start on C, then play G, then D, etc. See page 13 to review the cycle of 5ths.

2. Play the two exercises below.

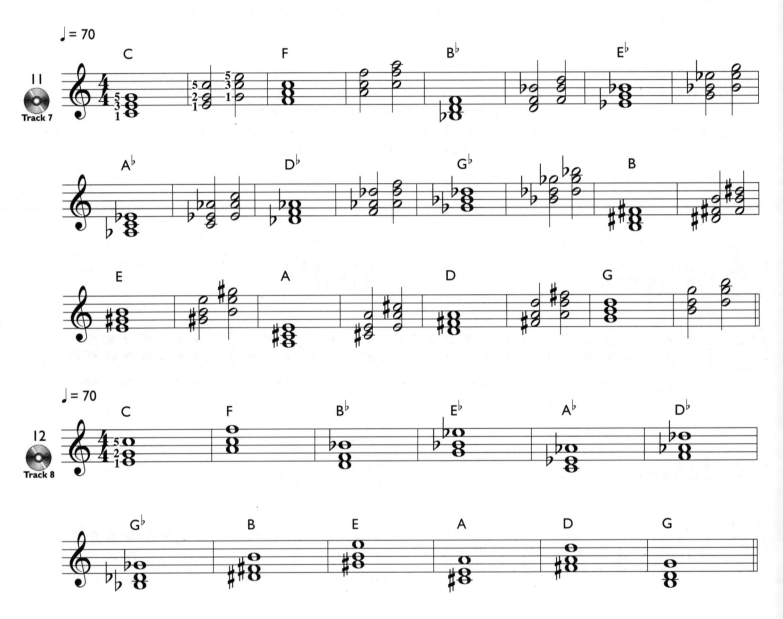

3. Following the format of example 12, play 2nd inversion triads through the cycle of 5ths, holding each chord for four beats.

Practice Tip:
- Play with a metronome. That way you are working on your rhythm all the time.
- Practice slowly. Give your ears and hand and brain time to absorb new information.
- Practice without looking at the page. These exercises are designed only to get you started. The blues is not a "reading" kind of music. It is most important to hear what you are doing.

It's time to get the left hand working harder. This is a typical *shuffle* bass pattern using triplets in the right hand. It also uses the triplet feel in the left hand, but instead of being notated as triplets it's shown as eighth notes with an indication that the eighths are *swung*. The marking, *Swing 8ths* means that the first eighth note of each beat is held longer than the second. Imagine accenting the first and third of three triple eighth notes like you did on page 22.

Play through the next song with just your left hand.

Now you are ready to add the right-hand part. The right hand is playing three triple eighth notes triplets per beat. So, the second eighth note in the left hand coincides with the third eighth note in the right-hand triplet. If this seems tricky at first, don't worry. You will have lots of opportunity to practice it throughout this book, and it will become easy.

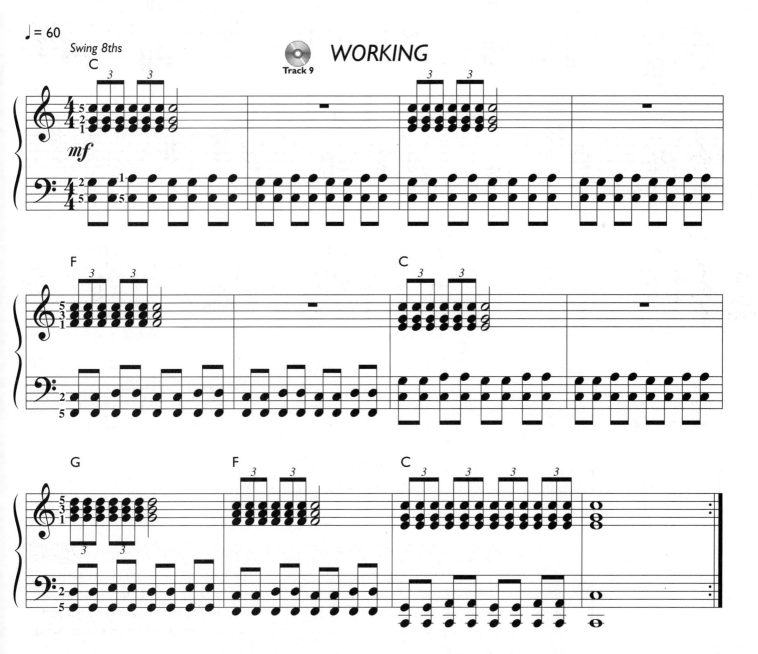

WORKING

Track 9

Practice this pattern through the descending cycle of 5ths. Here is an exercise to take you through six keys:

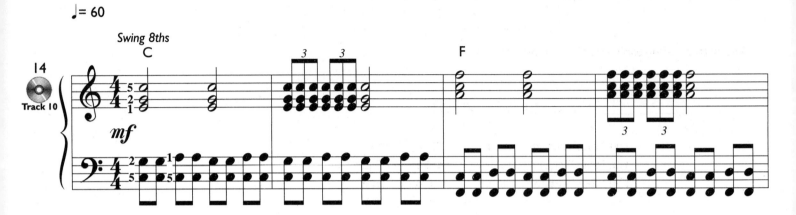

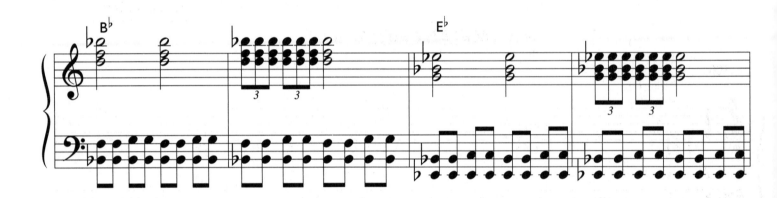

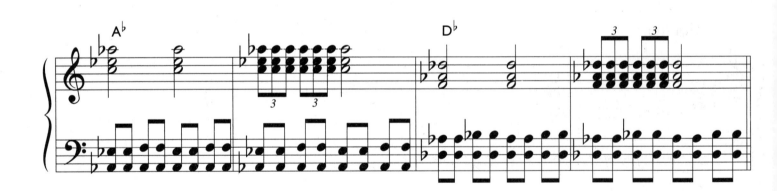

Now play the other six keys to finish the cycle of 5ths: G♭, B, E, A, D and G.

Sometimes the twelve-bar blues is played in a minor key. Look at what happens when we take diatonic triads from the natural minor to make a twelve-bar blues.

Let's start with the key of A Minor:

A	B	C	D	E	F	G
1	2	3	4	5	6	7

The pattern of diatonic triads for minor keys is:

i ii° III iv v VI VII

The "one" chord	i	will be A Minor
The "four" chord	iv	will be D Minor
The "five" chord	v	will be E Minor

Here is a minor blues using inversions of minor triads. Play the bass line alone first.

p = Piano. Soft.

MELANCHOLY BLUE
Track 11

This minor blues has an eighth-note pattern in the left hand which is played in straight eighths rather than swung. This means that all the eighth notes are of equal time value. The resulting feel is more like funk or rock.

Remember, the key of C Minor has three flat notes: B♭, E♭ and A♭.

Notice how almost all of the melody notes in this blues outline the minor triads. In the next chapter we will look at blues melodies in more detail. Your left hand is introduced to a new bass line. It is comprised entirely of roots, but in alternating octaves. This type of bass line is very common.

FUNKY THUNKY

Track 12

𝒇 = Forte. Loud.

Exercise:

Transpose this blues into the key of A Minor. Start by writing out the chord progression (use Roman numerals). Your left hand will play the roots of the chords. Your right hand will mainly outline inversions of the triads. You're on your way to playing the blues in twelve keys!

MAJOR CHORDS IN THE MINOR BLUES

A minor blues always starts on a minor chord, but quite often the V chord is major instead of minor, and sometimes both the IV and the V chords are major. This is the case in the next blues, which uses the same shuffle bass line we learned on page 25. The feel for this blues is swing eighths. Both the melody and the bass line are swung.

Look out—this blues is in B Minor, one of the saddest keys.

WORRYING BLUES

Track 13

Without thinking about it, you probably noticed that a minor blues has a darker, or sadder sound than a major blues. Different musical sounds evoke different emotional responses in us. It's important to learn to trust your instincts about sound so you will choose what you play to convey a feeling, rather than to follow a rule.

It's time to be the composer and write your own blues tune.

Below is a list of all the concepts we've been talking about. Choose any of them for your blues composition.

Major triads

Minor triads

Triads in first or second inversion

Straight eighth-note feel vs. swing eighths

Playing constant eighth-note triplets

Making triads into a melody (arpeggiation)

Bass lines:
    Playing the root
    Playing the root in octaves
    Shuffle style bass line

A few questions to get you started:

Will it be major or minor?
    (If minor, will the IV and V chords be minor or major?)
What key will it be in?
Which feel will the bass line have? Swing or Straight Eighths?
Will the right hand play chords, a single-note melody or both?
What will be the inversion of the first chord?

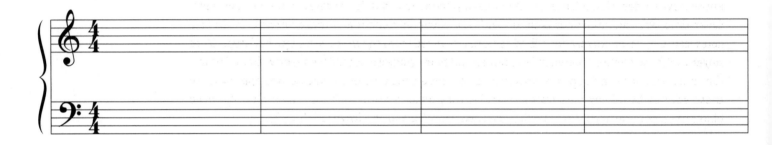

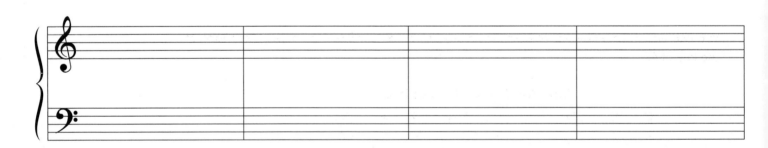

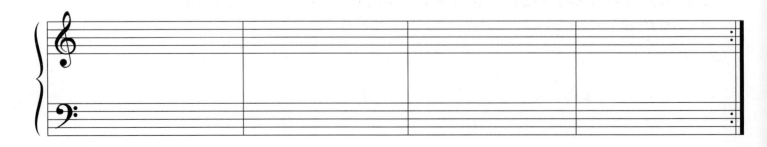

CHAPTER 3

Blues Melodies

Let's investigate how blues melodies are made. First of all, we have to remember that the blues developed as vocal music. The whole point of playing the blues is having a story or feeling to communicate. If we think about singing a song as we create a blues melody, we cannot go too far wrong.

Secondly, you have learned that the blues form has a specific sound. The combination of blues harmonies with certain melody notes creates sounds which clearly say "I've got the blues." In this chapter, you will become familiar with these sounds so that, in making blues melodies, you can capture the feeling that best tells your story.

We saw earlier that, by arpeggiating triads, it's possible to compose a blues melody solely from chord tones. This is fine, and as a starting point it's good to notice that *chord tones work as melody notes*. However, our goal is to get to the heart of the blues, and we wouldn't get very far with only the root, 3rd and 5th.

When people with backgrounds in European music first heard the blues being sung, they didn't know how to describe it because they heard pitches that didn't fit scales as they knew them. Over time, African influences blended with European influences and these pitches, called *blue notes*, came to be uniformly described as notes lowered from the major scale by a half step. Blues singers still sang pitches "between" the notes, and blues guitarists would frequently "bend" notes. On an instrument like the piano, however, or on paper, the best one could do was approximate these sounds by adding blue notes to scales they already knew. There are commonly three blue notes: the lowered 3rd ($\flat$3), the lowered 5th ($\flat$5), and the lowered 7th ($\flat$7).

In the key of **C** the notes are:	C	D	E	F	G	A	B
The blue notes are:			E$\flat$		G$\flat$		B$\flat$

We end up with a whole lot of notes to choose from for our blues melodies. Let's look at the key of C:

Notes for Blues Melodies in C									
C	D	(E$\flat$)	E	F	(G$\flat$)	G	A	(B$\flat$)	C
1	2	($\flat$3)	3	4	($\flat$5)	5	6	($\flat$7)	1

Some people call all of these notes together the *blues scale*. However, the term "blues scale" is more often used to refer to a subset of these notes. There are a few simpler scales contained within this group of notes and you will become familiar with them in this chapter.

Bessie Smith, "Empress of the Blues," was an extraordinary talent. A strong, hypnotic performer, Bessie was so good at conjuring her audience that her style was compared to Southern preachers. At the same time, she was capable of working with the finest jazz musicians, and is credited with moving the blues from a rural-countrified art form to a more sophisticated and urban blues-jazz blend. She rose from a childhood of extreme poverty and hardship to become the most popular black entertainer of her time.

PHOTO • COURTESY OF THE INSTITUTE OF JAZZ STUDIES

Drowning in My Blues is in the style of *Backwater Blues*, a classic Bessie Smith tune which has been covered by several other performers.

DROWNING IN MY BLUES

So much   sor-row on   my mind,———   Lord, I don't know what— to— do.

So much sor-row on   my mind,———   Lord, I don't know what- to— do.

'Cause it's   rain-ing— all the time———   I think I'm drown - ing in   my   blues.

* Go back to the first repeat sign and play again.

Notice the characteristic structure and content that make this a classic blues example.

• Three lyrical phrases. The first one is repeated. The third is a *response* to the first two.

• Three corresponding melodic phrases, set apart from each other by *space.*

• Each melodic phrase has a clear shape.

• Each melodic phrase contains chord tones and blue notes.

THE MAJOR PENTATONIC SCALE

Within the set of notes for blues melodies shown on page 31 are some more simplified scales, each of which gives a particular flavor to the blues. Two of these scales are the major and minor pentatonic scales. These scales get the name "pentatonic" from the fact that they are five-note scales. ("Penta" is the Greek word for "five." The major and natural minor scales are seven note scales.)

Here is the "formula" for the major pentatonic scale, along with the corresponding notes in the key of C:

1	2	3	5	6
C	D	E	G	A

The scale has a major sound because the 3rd, E, is a major 3rd (four half steps above the root—see the interval chart on page 12).

The best way to practice pentatonic scales on the keyboard is to play them over three octaves with fingerings that span two octaves.

TWO-OCTAVE FINGERINGS FOR MAJOR PENTATONIC SCALES

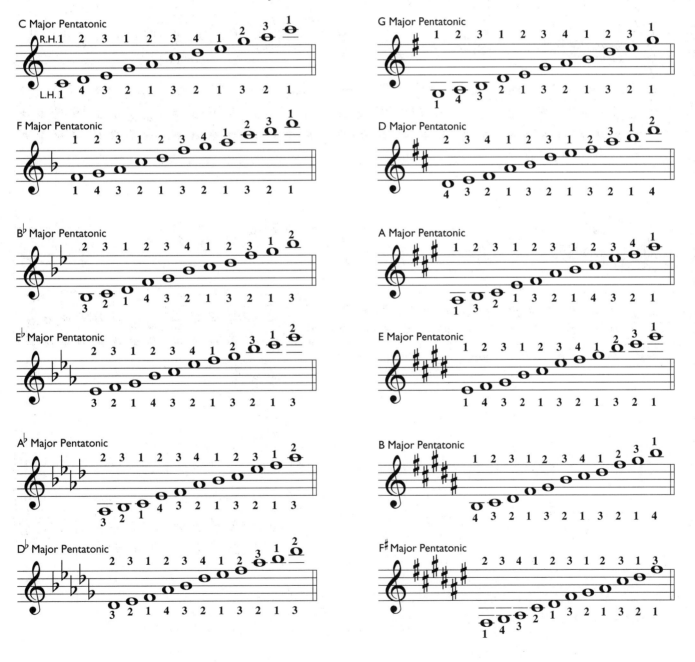

Here's a major blues for you to learn.

THE MAJOR'S BLUES

Track 14

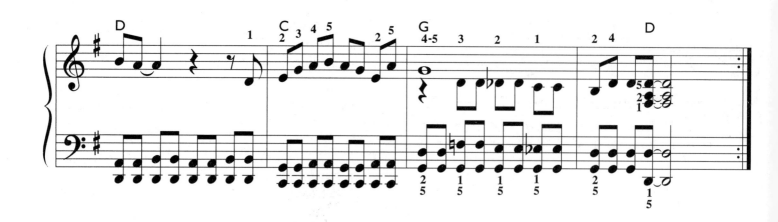

Just as for every major scale there is a relative minor scale (see page 14), for every major pentatonic scale there is a relative minor pentatonic scale. The root of the relative minor key is a 6th above the root of the major key.

Major Pentatonic Formula:	1	2	3	5	6	1
C Major Pentatonic:	C	D	E	G	A	C
A Minor Pentatonic:		A	C	D	E	G (A)

Numbering the notes of the minor pentatonic relative to its root gives us a new formula:

Let's find the notes of the C Minor Pentatonic:

A	C	D	E	G
1	♭3	4	5	♭7

C	E♭	F	G	B♭
1	♭3	4	5	♭7

The C Minor Pentatonic scale contains two blue notes for the key of C: E♭ and B♭. It also contains chord tones from all three triads used in a C blues progression. Listen to how a C blues sounds when the melody is taken from the C Minor Pentatonic scale.

THE MINER'S BLUES

Track 15

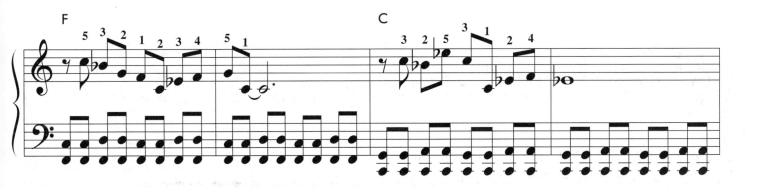

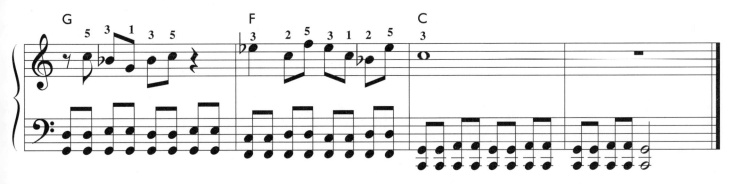

Review the pentatonic scale formula:

Minor Pentatonic Scale Formula
1 ♭3 4 5 ♭7

Major Pentatonic Scale Formula
1 2 3 5 6

Stevie Ray Vaughan came to prominence in the 1970s and '80s. He took soloing with pentatonic scales to new heights. Listen to his strongly minor pentatonic flavored playing on "Texas Flood" (Epic Records).

TWO-OCTAVE FINGERINGS FOR THE MINOR PENTATONIC SCALES

A Minor Pentatonic
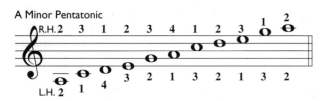

D Minor Pentatonic

G Minor Pentatonic
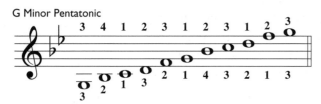

C Minor Pentatonic
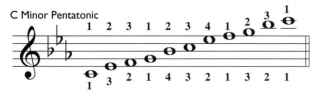

F Minor Pentatonic
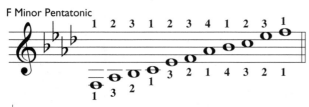

B♭ Minor Pentatonic
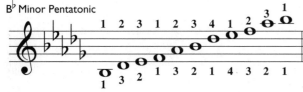

E Minor Pentatonic
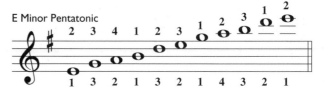

B Minor Pentatonic
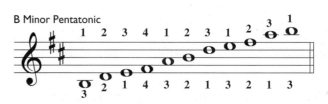

F♯ Minor Pentatonic
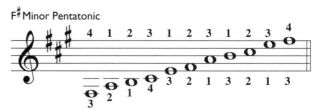

C♯ Minor Pentatonic
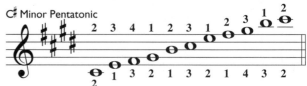

G♯ Minor Pentatonic
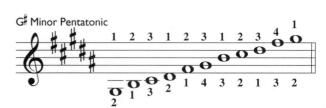

D♯ Minor Pentatonic
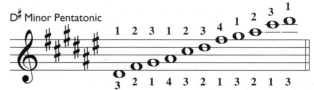

DOMINANT 7TH CHORDS

So far, the chords we've used to play the blues have been triads—three-note chords containing the root, 3rd and 5th of the scale they are from.

Now we're going to add one more note to the chords to make them 7th chords. Let's look at the notes of the major scale again, and this time, notice every other note:

C	D	**E**	F	**G**	A	**B**
1	2	**3**	4	**5**	6	**7**

We can use every other note of the scale to build a four-note chord:

C	E	G	B	
1	3	5	7	This is a **C Major 7** chord.

To make a C Dominant 7th chord, or **C7**, we lower the major 7th by a half step from B to B♭ (♭7).

C	E	G	B♭	
1	3	5	♭7	This is a **C7** chord.

Practice playing dominant 7th chords in root position around the cycle of 5ths. Play the root of each chord in your left hand.

This exercise gets you playing dominant chords in your left hand. Before you start, play a C7 chord with your left hand starting on C one octave below middle C on the piano. Now play C, E and B♭, but leave out the G. It sounds almost exactly the same, but less "muddy," or cluttered. Piano players have to be careful of playing too many notes, too close together in the lower ranges of the piano. Sometimes you can leave a note out of a chord, and still get the same sound. In this exercise you will leave out the 5th, playing only the 1, 3 and ♭7 of each chord.

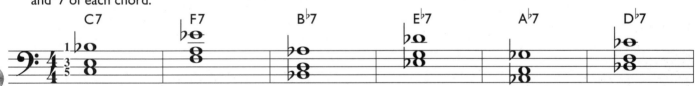

Another way to understand dominant 7th chords is to build them from the major scale in which their root is the 5th degree. For example, C is the 5th degree of F Major. So build a C7 chord by taking every other note of the F Major scale starting on C.

Position in scale:	1	2	3	4	5	6	7	1	2	3	4...
F Major scale:	F	G	A	B♭	C	D	E	F	G	A	B♭...
C7 chord:					C		E		G		B♭
Position in chord:					1		3		5		♭7

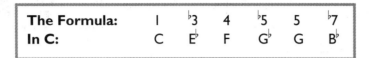

THE BLUES SCALE

We can make the minor pentatonic scale bluesier by adding one more note to it—the keyboard player's favorite blue note—the ♭5. This scale is often called *the blues scale*.

Here is the C Blues scale:

The Formula:	I	♭3	4	♭5	5	♭7
In C:	C	E♭	F	G♭	G	B♭

Since it includes all three blue notes, the ♭3, ♭5 and ♭7, this scale is going to provide you with a lot of great blues sounds. Some of your favorite licks will come out of this scale, so you should learn it very well in all twelve keys.

RIGHT-HAND FINGERINGS FOR THE BLUES SCALE IN TWELVE KEYS

Since the blues scale contains six notes, each one-octave fingering has either two groups of three (1-2-3, 1-2-3) or a group of two and a group of four (1-2,1-2-3-4). You can practice blues scales just like you practiced major scales (see the Practice Tip on the bottom of page 11).

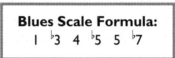

Blues Scale Formula:
I ♭3 4 ♭5 5 ♭7

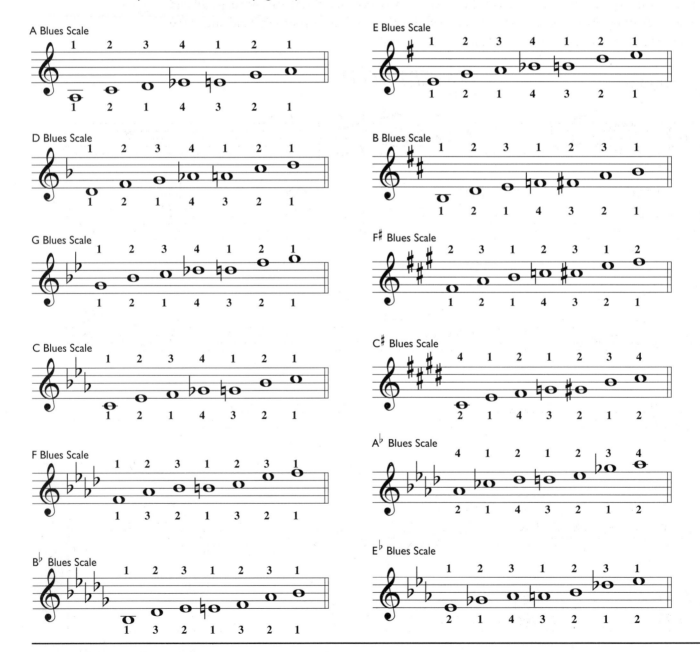

DOMINANT 7TH CHORDS AND THE BLUES SCALE

Dominant 7th chords create tension in a chord progression. Let's see why:

Within the notes of every dominant 7th chord is an interval called a *tritone*, which is another name for a diminished 5th or augmented 4th (a distance of six half steps).

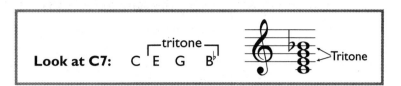

Look at C7: C E G B♭ (tritone from E to B♭) — Tritone

The interval from E to B♭ is a tritone. Played together, E and B♭ create a very *unresolved* or *tense* sound. Your ear wants to hear one or both of the notes move somewhere. Play E and B♭ together, then move each note in by one half-step to F and A.

You have just resolved the very unstable sound of a tritone to a stable sounding major 3rd. This type of resolution is the basis of most harmonic movement in our culture. Blues harmony is unique in that it frequently is based solely on dominant chords. The harmonic movement is from one dominant 7th chord to another and the tritone never fully resolves.

In this blues, you'll play dominant 7th chords in your left hand, and melodies from the blues scale in your right hand. In addition to the tension within each dominant 7th chord, you'll find some interesting dissonances (clashes) between the chord tones in your left hand and some of the right-hand melody notes. Welcome to the blues!

GET TO IT
Track 18

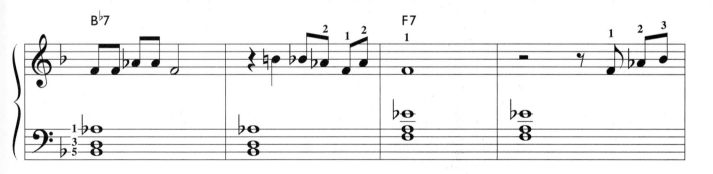

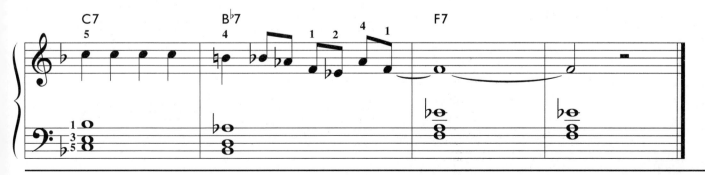

Observe what happens if we combine all the notes from the three dominant 7th chords in a C blues progression (C7—C, E, G, B♭; F7—F, A, C, E♭ and G7—G, B, D, F) and number them in relation to the key:

C	D	E♭	E	F	G	A	B♭	(B)
1	2	♭3	3	4	5	6	♭7	(7)

With the exception of B, all of these notes are found in either the C Major Pentatonic scale (C, D, E, G, A) or the C Minor Pentatonic scale (C, E♭, F, G, B♭).

> Blues melodies sound great with notes from both the major and minor pentatonic scales combined.

As you play through *Everything Blues*, notice which notes are from the major pentatonic scale and which are from the minor pentatonic scale.

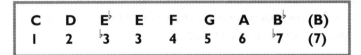

EVERYTHING BLUES

Track 19

TENSION AND RESOLUTION

In *Everything Blues* (page 40), you played nearly the same melody in the fifth bar as in the first, but the E natural was missing from the fifth bar. In its place is the note E♭. It sounds natural because the harmony changed from the I chord to the IV chord. The IV chord is F7, and the ♭7 of F7 is E♭. If we played an E natural over the F7 chord it would sound quite dissonant. (Try it. The E clashes with E♭ and with F.) So, we change our melody to fit the chord. This is one way in which we control the amount of tension in our melodies.

Go through the C blues progression one chord at a time. Over each chord, play the notes of the C Major Pentatonic and then the C Blues scale. First, determine which notes sound tense and which sound resolved over C7. Write your observations on a piece of scrap paper. Now do the same thing for F7. Do the same for G7. As you might have guessed, some notes that sound tense over C7 sound resolved over F7 and G7 and vice-versa.

And then there's the mighty ♭5. It sounds tense over *all* the chords. That's why it's the spiciest of all the blue notes. Usually we pass through it on the way up to the 5th or on our way down towards the root.

Here again are the notes from both the major and minor pentatonic scales combined:

Exercise:

Using combined notes from the C Major Pentatonic and C Blues scales, compose a phrase that begins on a tense note and ends on a resolved note for each chord of the C blues progression.

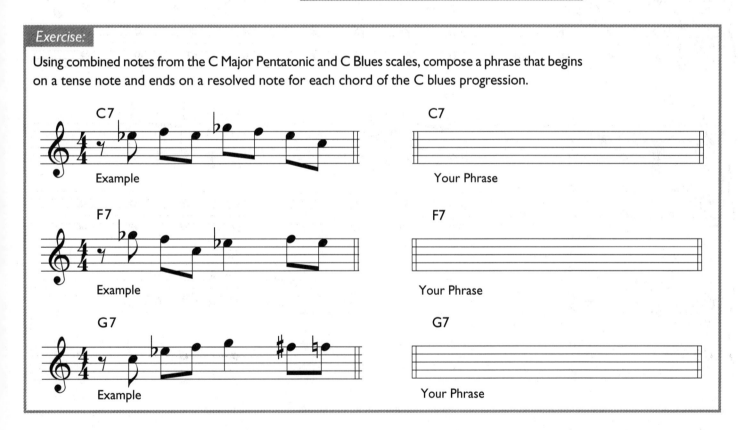

It is probably most difficult to write a phrase that sounds resolved over the V chord—in this case, G7. The V chord functions as the climax, or most unresolved point, in the chord progression. Because we are accustomed to harmonies that move in a cycle of 5ths, our ears want to hear the V chord resolve to I. We don't hear a resolution until we leave the V chord.

Once again, it's time for you to be the composer and experiment with creating blues melodies. In *C Blues*, there is an accompaniment provided. Using the CD that comes with this book, you'll be able to practice playing your own blues along with a rhythm section!

Remember, we have talked about three different scales that you can use:

major pentatonic

minor pentatonic

blues scale

Choosing notes from just one scale can be as effective as using notes from combined scales. Let your ear be your guide.

Here are a few other things to think about:

- Imagine that there are lyrics. You are telling a story, so remember to speak in clear sentences.
- Tension is ok. Just be sure to follow it with some resolution.
- Repetition and call and response are integral parts of the blues.
- Less is more. Space between phrases makes them stronger.

C BLUES

Track 20

CHAPTER 4

Playing a Shuffle

We already know from learning a shuffle-style bass line (page 25) that a shuffle is played with a triplet, or $\frac{12}{8}$ feeling, also called swing eighths. But there's a whole lot more to learn about the art of playing a shuffle. The shuffle has been developing for nearly a century now, with each great blues player along the way adding their signature to its evolution. In addition to the characteristic feel and bass patterns of shuffles, there are stylistic elements like *breaks*, *fills* and particular sounds that make a tune sound like a shuffle. You might hear a classic shuffle referred to also as a Chicago-style blues, because Chicago was the city where the great players played when the style was developing.

As a blues pianist, you get to play lots of different roles. You can be melodic, harmonic or rhythmic—or some combination of all three. When you play a solo shuffle on the piano, you actually fill many roles at once: you tell the story, you propel it forward with rhythm and you punctuate it. When you play with a singer or a band, you'll be trading roles with the other musicians, and will need to always find a niche to play in that will enhance the music. As you learn to play the blues, listen to both solo piano players and pianists with bands. Listen to how the piano player's role changes from situation to situation, and from moment to moment, within one song. That way, as you acquire more skills on the keyboard, you will be ready to use them musically.

In this chapter, we'll learn about the feeling of a shuffle, about when and how to fill up the spaces in a melody and about putting the icing on top of whatever else might be going on without getting in its way.

Eddie Boyd, was very active in the Chicago scene during the 1940s and '50s. Known for the sophistication of his playing, Eddie Boyd played briefly with Muddy Waters. He then went on to play with Sonny Boy Williamson's band. Boyd provided excellent accompaniment to Johnny Shines and Jimmy Rogers as well as recording his own tunes. His biggest hit was Five Long Years (J.O.B. Records) which topped the R&B charts in 1952.

PHOTO • BILL GREENSMITH

Here's a shuffle in F using another type of shuffle bassline. First, play the left hand alone and remember to swing the eighth notes. In your right hand, you'll be adding triplets. Since the bassline is swung, your left and right hands will play together on the first and third part of each triplet.

 CHICAGO TIME

Exercise:

- Go through this blues and notice where the ♭5 (C♭ or B♮) is being played. Play each phrase with a ♭5 in it a few times to get familiar with how it is used.
- Transpose this bassline into the key of C. It's easy, because the bassline outlines each chord the same way: R, 3, 5, 6, ♭7.

FUN WITH THE ♭5

In bars 9 and 10 of *Chicago Time* you played a figure that is very common in the blues: the ♭5, resolving to the 5. This figure sounds even better when you add the root on top.

Your right handthumb and second finger will alternate between the ♭5 and 5, while your pinkie repeats the root on top. Try it slowly.

Now play the exercise again, but move your right hand up one octave.

Sometimes your favorite blues licks will sound better in the higher ranges of the piano. If, for example, you play with guitar players, most of the guitar notes will be in a relatively low range. If you play figures in the low to middle range of the piano (around middle C) while the guitar player is in the same range, your sound will get lost, or it will add too much clutter to the sound. There will be too much going on in one range. But, if in the same situation, you play in the upper range of the keyboard, your sound will come through on the top. Of course, the guitar player might not like you playing something above what they are doing, but sometimes it's very effective. Use discretion. Listen to great players and then trust your ears.

Learn to find this common lick quickly and easily in all twelve keys. Here is an exercise taking it through four keys starting with E (a favorite key of guitar players). Continue through the cycle of 5ths.

Practice slowly and stop if you feel fatigued. It takes a little patience to get used to playing these repetitive figures smoothly.

We've learned two basslines that work for shuffles:

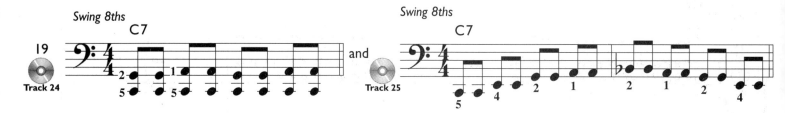

They have a few things in common: they are made up of swing eighths; they start on the root; and they outline the chords somehow. Notice that the 6th keeps showing up in these lines. You can think of the 6th in a couple of different ways. In the first pattern, it's substituting for the 7th. Using the 6 instead of the $\flat$7 gives the chord a more open sound—not specifically dominant. In the second example, the 6th is used as a passing tone on the way to the $\flat$7.

Here are a few more typical shuffle basslines:

Exercise:

Choose one of the basslines above and take it through a twelve-bar blues progression in the key of F.

The bass player in a blues band will sometimes play just the root of the chord on each beat of the bar, or in the swing eighth rhythm. In that case, it might be your role, or the guitar players role, to play one of the these shuffle patterns above the bass. Again, you have to use your ears to hear what works.

Flat Five Shuffle gives you some more practice with your new ♭5 lick, as well as a new bass line pattern.

FLAT FIVE SHUFFLE

Observe what's happening in the last bar. That little musical figure, and the G7 chord, is called a *turnaround*. A turnaround brings you back to the beginning of the form so you can play another *chorus* (once through the form is usually referred to as one chorus). We'll learn more about turnarounds a little later in this section.

TREMOLOS AND FILLS

You've heard them—maybe you've already played them. If you haven't, you undoubtedly want to. *Tremolos* in the right hand, over a nice shuffle groove, are an essential ingredient in the blues sound. A tremolo is a rapid alternation between two notes. Sometimes blues players will call this a *roll*.

There are a few different notes you can tremolo between that sound great. We'll start with the most obvious: **the root.**

You can tremolo between the root and the ♭3 of the key over almost the whole blues progression.

In the key of F: Put your thumb on F, and your 2nd or 3rd finger on A♭. Now roll your hand back and forth between the two notes. It might seem awkward at first, but it will become more natural as you keep working at it. The key is to keep your hand relaxed. If this technique is new to you, be careful not to overdo it in the beginning. It is better to practice new techniques for a few moments frequently, rather than trying to sit down and master something all at once.

This is how tremolos or rolled notes are notated in the written music:

 Tremolo on F and A♭ for 5 beats.

The next song will help you develop this new technique.

Notice what happened in bar 9. That little F♯ is an enharmonic respelling of the ♭5 (G♭) in the key of C, which is the chord you are playing over in that bar. Play the F♯ quickly with the C and slide to the G, the 5 in the key of C. Some people call this a *crush tone* or a *grace note*. We'll do more of this in the next few chapters.

_____

CHAPTER 5

Piano Blues Sounds

The piano can be the most exciting instrument to play, as well as the most challenging, because it can be so many things. It's a melodic instrument, a harmonic instrument and a percussion instrument all rolled into one. In no style of music is this more evident than the blues. As we further explore the art of blues piano, it will become more difficult to draw clear lines between what's the melody, what's the harmony and what's adding to the groove. It will become important to think in terms of "piano blues sounds" and develop a whole vocabulary of sounds that you can put together in order to get just the right feeling.

PHOTO • COURTESY OF THE INSTITUTE OF JAZZ STUDIES

Otis Spann is considered by many to be the greatest blues ensemble pianist ever. In 1952 Otis Spann was introduced to Muddy Waters by Len Chess, and joined Muddy in what would become a history-making band. Spann's solid, powerful playing style was derived in large part from Maceo Merriweather, who was on the Chicago scene before him. But Otis's unique contribution to the art was in finding the perfect way to make his bold sounds enhance but never intrude upon the new sounds of the Chicago blues.

We learned a bit about classic blues sounds, such as the ♭3 tremolo and the ♭5 lick, in Chapter 4. In this chapter, we'll focus on more piano blues sounds and how to use them. There is perhaps no one better to inspire an appetite for these sounds than Otis Spann. Listen to nearly any Otis Spann cut and you will hear wrenching blue-note clusters, driving trills and cascading blues riffs explode from his piano. He uses the piano to help tell a story, which is what the blues is all about.

In the pre-electric and early electric days of the blues, pianists like Otis Spann were playing unamplified pianos in noisy clubs and had to find ways of being heard. This led to the development of techniques to make big sounds. Licks were frequently played in the high ranges of the piano, notes were tremoloed or played in octaves and dissonant *clusters* (groups of notes a major or minor 2nd apart played simultaneously) were barked out in the guitar breaks. These sounds are still an integral part of playing the style. A good blues keyboardist needs to know exactly how and when to use them in order to enhance the music.

OTIS'S BLUES

Track 31

The most important part of learning the blues is listening. It's time for you to start shopping around for your own favorite sounds on recordings. Listen to Otis Spann solo or with Muddy Waters' incredible band. Check out Maceo Merriweather, Lafayette Leake, Memphis Slim, Meade Lux Lewis and Jimmy Yancey. Stop your recording at the spot that grabs you the most and see if you can figure out what sound the piano player is playing. If you don't already have many blues recordings, there are some great blues piano compilations available which will give you a sampling (see the discography on page 96). You can also find classic blues recordings in your library.

THREE-NOTE ♭5 LICK

Let's take a look at what you were playing when you played *Otis's Blues* on page 50. The first line starts out with a classic Otis Spann sound played as a cluster. The notes are A♯, B and D. In relation to the key of E, these are the ♭5, the 5 and the ♭7—three notes out of the E Blues scale. In the first two bars they're played as a cluster, and in the third bar they are arpeggiated, which we know means played one at a time. Both of these ways of playing the ♭5, 5 and ♭7 sound great over the blues progression in any key. You should know where these notes are in every key and be able to grab them quickly.

Exercise:

Play the following four-bar figure in all twelve keys, moving through the keys in ascending 4ths (or downward 5ths). In your left hand, play the first basic shuffle pattern we learned. In your right hand play the ♭5, 5 and ♭7 for that key. Experiment with playing the notes individually, as a repeated cluster, or try trilling them. Here are a few keys to get you started:

In the tenth bar of *Otis's Blues*, you played what might be the most well-known of all blues piano licks. For this lick, we use the first four notes of the blues scale: the root, the ♭3, 4 and ♭5. This lick is almost always played using sixteenth notes (or notes with an even shorter rhythmic value.)

Let's learn this lick using sixteenth notes. This means there are four notes for every beat. Even though we are swinging the eighth notes when we play a shuffle, we will give each sixteenth note equal rhythmic value. Try playing this lick in the key of E, to a metronome set at 60.

When you can play it smoothly, turn the metronome faster a few clicks at a time, playing the lick at each new tempo. When you are comfortable at 80 or 90 beats per minute, try adding the shuffle pattern in your left hand. Remember to keep the swing feel in your left hand, but try to play all the sixteenth notes equally in your right hand. Practicing each hand separately with a metronome until it is very comfortable will help you to put the two hands together.

> *Exercise:*
>
> In the keys of E and A, play your new blues lick through the entire blues progression using sixteenth notes in your right hand and any of the shuffle patterns we've learned in your left hand. Although you might want to play the right-hand lick even faster (in other words, with notes shorter than sixteenth notes), keep it to sixteenth notes at first. It is important to learn to play different rhythmic patterns with control (confidence and accuracy). The cool rhythmic stuff you'll want to play down the road will only sound cool if you learn habits of control now.

Blues pianists use *octave doublings* for volume and dramatic effect. For a great example of this, listen to Chicago Pianist Lafayette Leake playing behind Howlin' Wolf on the tune *Louise* (Chess Records). The descending octaves on the piano becomes an integral part of the arrangement.

If you have not worked a lot on piano technique, or tried to play octaves before, they might seem difficult at first. As with any new technique, it's important to start slowly and stay relaxed.

Let's begin in E, by playing the root in octaves:

Now try this simple lick from the blues scale:

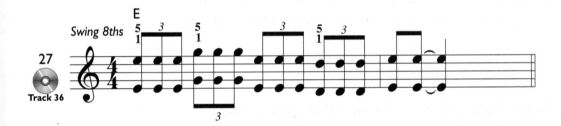

Once the exercises above are comfortable, try playing the whole blues scale in octaves.

Ascending...

...and descending.

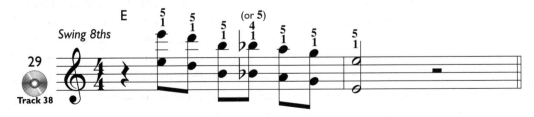

Undersung pianist **Lafayette Leake** played with a host of Chicago blues guitarists and vocalists in the 1950s and '60s including Otis Rush's and Muddy Water's main rival for attention on the Chicago scene, Howlin' Wolf (Chester Burnett).

LAFAYETTE'S BLUES

Track 39

PHOTO • BILL GREENSMITH

Major "Big Maceo" Merriweather came up during the boogie-woogie craze, and went on to become one of the most popular blues artists on the Chicago scene in the 1940s. Maceo's piano style was hugely influential to the young pianists coming up in Chicago, most notably two of Muddy Waters' pianists: Little Johnny Jones and Otis Spann.

Maceo sang and played, and his songs were mainly his own, many of them in the sixteen-bar blues form. His most well-known song is Worried Life Blues, *which borrowed a verse from guitarist Sleepy John Estes. Maceo's first recording session took place in 1941, and unfortunately his last was in 1945. Shortly after that time, Maceo suffered a paralyzing stroke, and though he recovered from it, he never again reached the place in his playing that he left. The 1945 session produced Maceo's solo masterpiece,* Chicago Breakdown, *a classic example of boogie-woogie piano at its finest.*

Frequently, a minor blues will be a funky or jazzy blues, with a whole different feel from a shuffle or delta blues. There are blues tunes, however, that sound similar to *Otis's Blues* (page 50), except that the i chord is minor. In these cases the form is usually i, IV, V. For example, in the key of F, the chords in the progression would be Fmin, B♭7 and C7. Since the sounds we've been working on in this chapter come from the blues scale, which is mainly the minor pentatonic, they'll work fine over a blues with a i, IV7, V7 progression. Below is an example of a minor blues shuffle. It includes sounds you know, but puts them into a slightly different context.

This blues is in the style of a very successful tune that left-handed guitarist and vocalist Otis Rush recorded for Chess Records called *So Many Roads*.

> *A *pickup* is a note (or notes) that occur before the first full measure of a piece.

RUSH'S ROADS

Track 40

PLAYING OFF OF TRIADS

In Chapter 3, you learned that we can alter blues melodies to fit the chords as they change (page 41). Let's take that concept one step further and consider playing deliberately "off of" each chord.

Here is a way of playing off of triads that might be the most frequently played keyboard sound in popular music:

If you wanted to analyze it harmonically, you could say it's a quick I-IV-I progression with the IV chord in second inversion, and the I chord in root position (see the triads review on page 16, and the section on triad inversions on page 23). Every chord in the blues is then treated as a I-IV-I. Alternatively, you could just think of it as tension-resolution—moving away from the chord tones and then coming back.

BENDING THE 3RD

When we play these figures off of triads, it's nice to add the ♭3 as a *grace note* preceding the 3rd. A grace note is a quick ornamental note played directly before the main note. Some of us call this *bending the 3rd* because it sounds similar to a guitar player bending a note. It feels more natural in some keys than in others, depending upon where the black notes and white notes fall under your fingers. Here's how it works:

If the ♭3 is a black note, and the 3 is a white note, as in the keys of C, F or G, you can simply slide your 2nd finger from the ♭3 to the 3.

If the ♭3 is a white note, and the 3 is a black note, it's a little more awkward. Try playing the ♭3 with your 2nd finger and the 3 with your 3rd finger.

You'll find that you gravitate to certain sounds in certain keys, and each key will have its own vocabulary for that reason. It's a good idea, however, to practice each new sound in all twelve keys. It helps you to learn the sound really well—and sometimes you will have to play in G♭ on a gig!

Triad Blues gives you some practice with the device you just learned. Although it is not indicated in the music, go ahead and try bending the 3rd of each chord. In this case, all the ♭3s are black notes and all the 3s are white notes, so you can slide your 2nd finger from ♭3 to 3.

TRIAD BLUES

Track 44

> **Exercise:**
>
> Try to play through *Triad Blues* in the key of F.   The I will be F, the IV will be B♭ and the V will be C. Bending the 3rd for the IV (B♭) chord is a little trickier than it was in C (where the IV is F). All the notes will be a perfect 4th higher. Try it, but remember, bending notes is an aesthetic choice. You don't need to do it all the time. Sometimes, you might want to just play the chord cleanly.

PLAYING OFF THE DOMINANT 7TH CHORD

In the same way that we played off of triads, we can play figures off of dominant 7th chords.

Let's look again at the figure you just played off of a triad:

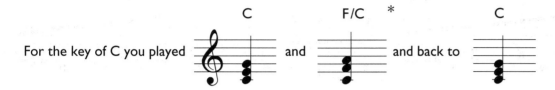

For the key of C you played [C] and [F/C *] and back to [C]

Instead of returning to the triad (C, E and G), move the note F up a whole step to G and the note A up a half step to B♭. You are playing the root, 5th and ♭7th of a C7 chord.

Try playing this sequence that starts from the top and goes down:

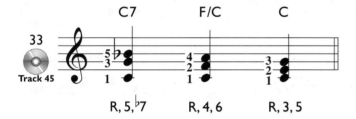

33 Track 45

> * This is called a *slash chord*. The letter to the left of the slash is the name of the chord. The letter to the right of the chord is the name of the note on the bottom. This is a convenient way to indicate a chord inversion, or the presence of a non-chord tone in the bass.

Now try the same thing starting with a G7 chord:

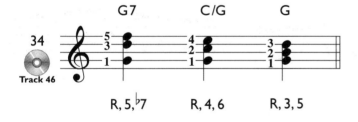

34 Track 46

With a D7 chord, let's start from the triad and go up to the dominant 7th chord:

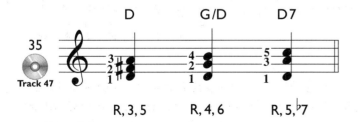

35 Track 47

Dominant Blues will give you some practice with playing off the dominant 7th chords.

DOMINANT BLUES

Track 48

CHAPTER 6

A Look at Boogie-Woogie

Boogie-woogie piano was one of the earliest blues piano styles to develop. It was the result of the combined influences of ragtime piano and "barrelhouse" playing (a rougher or cruder version of ragtime which featured heavy left-hand playing known as stomping). Boogie-woogie was characterized by forceful left-hand bass figures which featured repetitive and often fast eight-to-the bar rhythms (a feel in which all the eighth notes are given equal weight). Volume and momentum are important aspects of boogie-woogie playing, and it is perhaps for this reason that bass lines with octave doublings frequently appeared. Many historians think boogie-woogie emerged from the South, as did Clarence "Pine Top" Smith who made the boogie style famous with his 1928 recording of *Pine Top's Boogie-Woogie* for Vocalian records. The boogie-woogie craze subsided by the 1950s as electric blues bands like Muddy Waters' changed the sound of the blues. But the influence of boogie-woogie piano on the blues continued to be great. In 1986, boogie-woogie legend Jimmy Yancey was inducted into the Rock and Roll Hall of Fame as the one who "gave rock its roll."

Boogie Blues on page 62 is a boogie-woogie tune in C. The feel is a little different from a shuffle. The tempo is faster than the shuffles you have been playing, and the eighth notes are not swung as hard. In other words, the eighth notes will become closer to straight eighths. Remember that straight eighths get equal rhythmic value, while in swing eighths the first of each pair is held longer than the second.

Practice this tune slowly with a metronome, then increase the tempo a click or two at a time until it is up to the metronome marking.

Clarence "Pine Top" Smith
might be considered the father of boogie-woogie. His influence gave rise to pianists like Jimmy Yancey, Meade Lux Lewis, Albert Ammons, Charles "Cow-Cow" Davenport and Pete Johnson. Pine Top's Boogie Woogie, *one of the most influential blues recordings of all time, was a dance piece. Pine Top himself was an all-around entertainer who sang and tap danced in addition to playing the piano. His recording days were short-lived—at age twenty-five he was accidentally shot during a dispute in the Masonic lodge where he was playing.*

BOOGIE BLUES

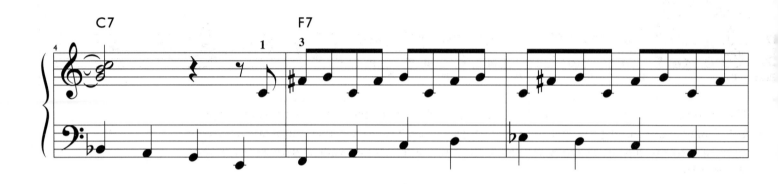

Let's review eighth-note feels, using the melody from *Boogie Blues*.

You'll play the first line of the melody three times with your metronome set to 80.

The first time, play the eighth notes straight:

The second time, play the line as you did for a shuffle—swinging the eighth notes in a triplet feel:

The third time, try to play the melody in a feel somewhere between straight eighths and triplet feel. Think about making the first note of each pair just a little longer than the second. Don't worry if it seems difficult, at this point you are just trying to increase your understanding of the different feels.

BOOGIE-WOOGIE BASS LINES

A boogie-woogie bass line has either four or eight notes per bar. It either outlines the chords or "walks." In either case it might contain repeated notes, or notes repeated an octave away.

Look at the bass line you just played for *Boogie Blues* (page 62). The notes are similar to other bass lines you have played, but the feel is different. For a shuffle, your left hand plays eighth notes with a triplet feel, while your right hand either played triplets, or swung the eighths along with your left. In this boogie bass line, you play quarter notes instead of eighth notes. That leaves the right hand free to play the eighths note a little more evenly. At quicker tempos, the eighth notes will sound almost straight.

To make this bass line into an eighth-note line in a boogie style, we could add octaves:

Walking the bass means that instead of just playing chord tones in the bass line, you connect the chord tones with scale tones, taking smaller steps between notes. You "walk" up the scale from which the chord is built.

Here is *Boogie Blues* again with a simple walking bass line. For each chord, the bass line uses the first three notes of the scale that the chord is taken from.

 ## WALKING BOOGIE BLUES

We can make our walking boogie bass line an eighth-note line, by adding octaves:

> *Exercise:*
> Play through *Walking Boogie Blues* one more time using the walking line with octaves.

Just as for other blues styles, boogie-woogie can be in a major or minor key. Here is a minor boogie that uses the same type of walking bass line you just played. Since the chords are minor, the notes in the bass line come from a minor scale.

This tune uses minor 7th chords (min7). To make a minor 7th chord, take the formula for a dominant 7th chord (1, 3, 5, ♭7) and flat the 3rd (1, ♭3, 5, ♭7).

I	♭3	5	♭7
C	E♭	5	♭7

This is a Cmin7 chord.

Cmin7

 SO LONG BOOGIE

Track 55

Almost Straight 8ths

♩=120 Amin

Dmin7   Amin

Emin   Dmin   Amin

We could also turn this walking boogie line upside down, walking down from the root rather than up. Let's keep the octaves. The chords are min7 chords, so the next note down from the root will be a whole step below the root (the ♭7).

Amin   Dmin

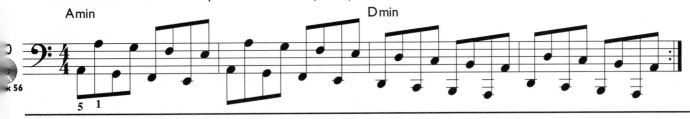

In *Boogie Train*, your right hand provides some forward momentum. Right-hand boogie parts were often simple and repetitive. The most important part of boogie-woogie is always the rhythm. Play just the right hand part to *Boogie Train* several times, then add the left hand. Play the eighth notes with an almost straight feel.

BOOGIE TRAIN

Track 57

JIMMY YANCEY-STYLE BOOGIE-WOOGIE

The right-hand part you played in *Boogie Train* is similar to what Jimmy Yancey might have played on a boogie tune. However, now that you've gotten used to thinking about playing the eighths straighter, we are going to complicate things by playing a Jimmy Yancey style of boogie which, like a shuffle, is played in a triplet feel!

Try the bass line alone first:

The right-hand part is the same as what you played for *Boogie Train*, with some *leading tones* added. Leading tones are notes in a melody or bass line that don't necessarily come from the chord or the scale from which the chord is built, but are used to approach a chord tone. This relates to issues of tension and resolution discussed in Chapter 3. Leading tones are a half-step above or below chord tones and always resolve to chord tones.

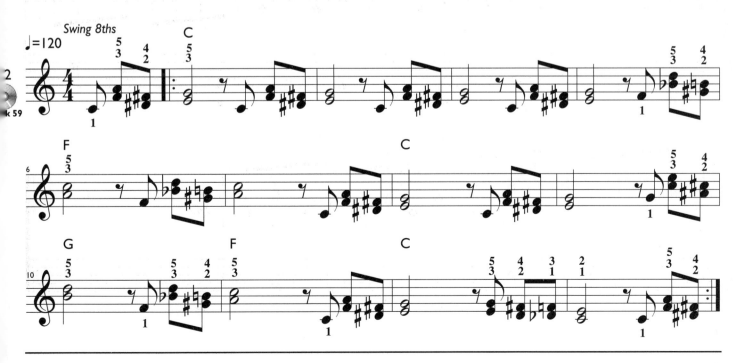

It's time to put the two parts together.

JIMMY'S BOOGIE

Track 60

James Edward "Jimmy" Yancey is thought
by many to be the master of boogie-woogie,
but his quiet stage demeanor did not lend
itself to stardom, and he did not tour or record
as prolifically as his own protogées. On
the bandstand, Jimmy frequently provided
accompaniment to his wife, a vocalist, Estelle
"Mama" Yancey. Despite Jimmy Yancey's
subdued nature, his music was part of the boogie-
woogie craze. Jimmy Yancey is respected by both
blues and jazz enthusiasts as a master of his art.

CHAPTER 7

Rhythm, Comping, Playing in a Band

Piano players such as Otis Spann and Pinetop Perkins, who played with Muddy Waters, came up with the perfect piano parts to accentuate the groove, support or punctuate a solo or just enhance the overall sound. When you play blues piano with a band, you will have to do the same. You will be faced with certain aesthetic choices, and will need a varied palette of rhythmic, harmonic and melodic tools to draw from in order to make good choices.

PHOTO • COURTESY OF STAR FILE, INC.

Muddy Waters, the King of the Chicago blues scene in the 1950s, surrounded himself with extraordinary musicians. He put together history-making bands with vocals, guitar, harmonica, piano, bass and drums. Muddy's bands played a blues style that was firmly based in country blues, but the originality and sophistication of their sound, and their arrangements, moved the style significantly forward.

COMPING

Comping is a word that comes from the word "accompaniment." Musicians use "comping" as a catch-all term for what piano players or guitar players play behind a soloist. Basically, to *comp* is to play the chords.

When comping, you deal with three elements of music: rhythm, harmony and melody. Over the next few pages, we will deal with knowing what chords to play (harmony), having control over where you want to put them in the time (rhythm) and making the chord motion sound good (melody). If you master your comping skills, you will make the band sound great and be in demand!

Let's start with a simple comping exercise using triads. Your left hand plays on the first and third beats of each bar, while your right hand plays on two and four.

BLUES IN G

Track 61

Exercise:

Transpose the above exercise into the key of F. Determine the inversions used for the I, IV and V chords.

The triads in the *Blues in G* (page 70) were in certain inversions to create good voice leading. Notice how the top note stayed the same when you moved from the I chord to the IV chord (measure 4 and 5). Also, the top note of your voicings for the whole first eight bars was the root of the key. You can almost never go wrong with the root as the top note of your chord. Keeping this idea in mind will help you play more complex chords and progressions.

In *Comping in D*, you will use the same pattern of inverted triads, but your right hand will play a dotted-quarter rhythm (see page 21).

COMPING IN D

Track 62

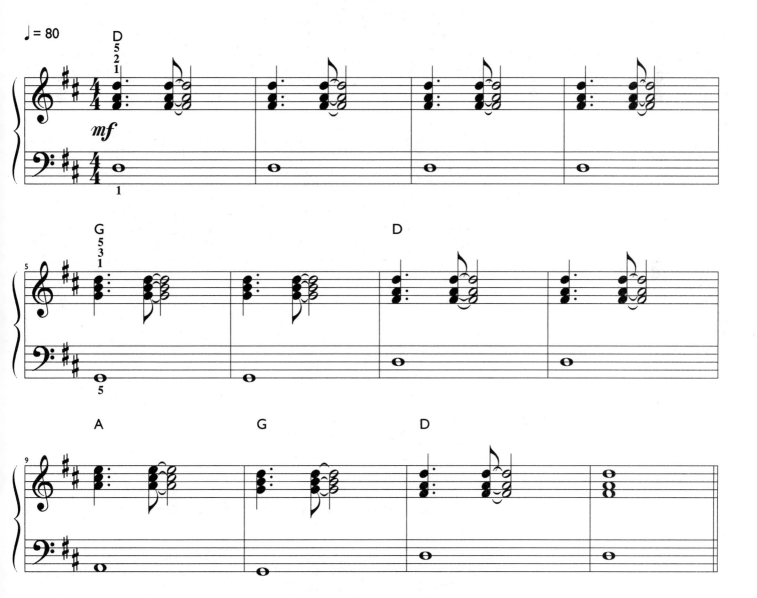

Now that you're comfortable with that rhythm, we're going to make the left hand work a little harder. Your left hand is going to play the first shuffle pattern you learned (page 25). Swing the eighths. Instead of just counting the beats, think about playing the shuffle patter in your left hand and then adding your right. Your hands should line up on the first beat of every bar and the "and of 2" of every bar. Another way to think of it is that your right hand plays the second chord of each bar together with the fourth note of your left hand.

COMPING SHUFFLE IN D

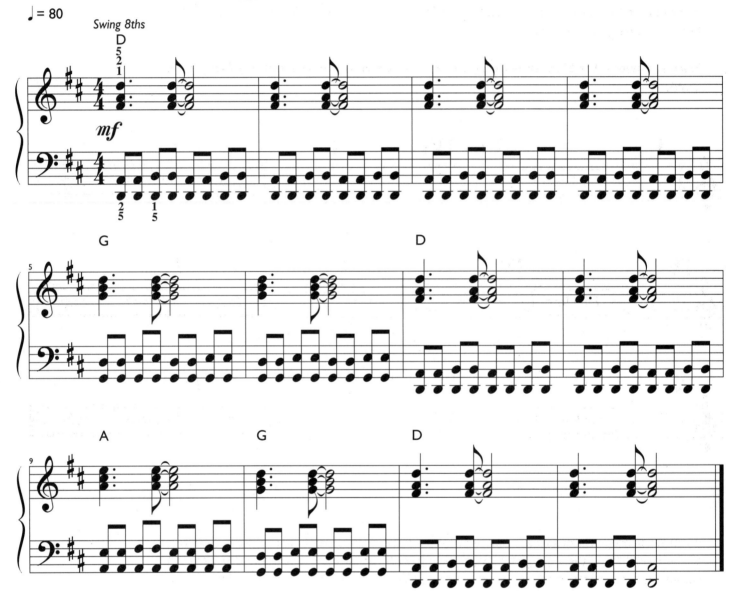

Track 63

> *Exercise:*
>
> Let's assume that our shuffle just became an uptempo boogie-woogie or rock-and-roll tune. Play through the same exercise again, exactly as written, but play the eighth notes almost straight with the metronome set at 120.

THE BEAUTY OF FILLS

When you listen to a great blues singer sing or guitarist play, they always leave space between phrases. A great blues band does brilliant things with that space. This is where *fills* come in. The fills in a blues tune can be almost as important as the phrases they fall between. Think of fills as being affirmation and punctuation of what the soloist is saying.

Johnnie Jones played with a great Chicago guitarist/vocalist named Elmore James. James played a song called *Dust My Broom*. The way the fills fell in that song became a format upon which many blues tunes were based. Listen to *Dust My Broom* to get a good feeling for the interplay between voice, guitar and band.

Here is a twelve-bar blues showing where fills might typically fall in a *Dust My Broom* style shuffle.

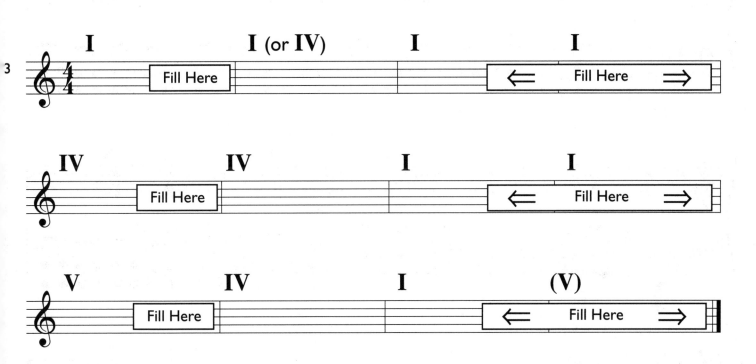

If you are playing behind a vocalist and there is no guitar, then it might be up to you to provide all the right fills. If there's a guitar player, you have to be ready to react with just the right commentary to everything they play or don't play. Your fills can be made up of all the different piano blues sounds we've talked about—trills, clusters, ♭5 licks, etc.

Guitar Player is a shuffle in C. There is a melody part written for guitar (in small, cue-sized notes) so that you get a chance to be the fill-master. You can play along with the CD that comes with this book, or start hanging out with some fellow blues players and working on these concepts together. Communication with other musicians is the most important musical skill you can have.

GUITAR PLAYER

COMPING WITH OCTAVES

You don't always have to play all of the notes in the chords. In fact, if someone else is already comping, or playing a very dense solo right in the midrange (like a guitar player) you could choose to lay out completely, or play something with a more open sound.

One way to add to the groove without cluttering the sonic space is to play a repeated rhythmic figure in octaves.

In *Octavia*, your right hand plays a rhythm that is typical of what a horn section might play. Again, you will have to subdivide to eighth notes to count the rhythm. Make sure to note the beats on which your right hand plays.

Exercise:

After you have mastered *Octavia*, play through it again with your right hand one octave higher than written. A great thing about the tradition of blues piano is that you get to use the whole range of the piano. Have fun with it.

Since much of blues harmony is based on the sound of dominant 7th chords, it's important to be very familiar with them in every key. Good voice leading is something you'll always want to strive for, and that means you need to be able to easily invert dominant 7th chords.

Since dominant 7th chords have four notes, they have four positions.

Let's look at a C7 chord:

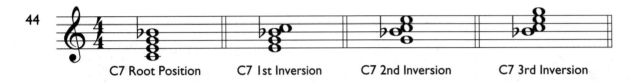

Play through the following exercise to familiarize yourself with all the dominant 7th chord positions in all keys. Something to notice: with the exception of root position, you will always have a whole step between the dominant 7th and the root in your voicing. Try it with your left hand, too.

Now continue down through the second half of the cycle of 5ths. Don't forget, guitar players like to play in sharp keys like A and E, so don't ignore them!

VOICE LEADING WITH DOMINANT 7TH CHORDS

Now we can use inverted dominant 7th chords to comp through a blues in G, using a classic rhythm that will work over a swing or straight eighth feel. Because we know it sounds good, we'll start with the root (G), as the top note of the chord.

There's no left hand part written here. Sometimes, when you're comping in a band, it sounds too cluttered if you play with both hands. Focus only on your right hand for a few times then, if you wish, try it together with a simple left hand shuffle pattern.

(1) & (2 &) 3 (& 4 &)   1 (& 2)   &   (3 & 4 &)

Exercise:

Let's try putting the 5th in the top voice of the first chord. The 5th of G7 is D, so our first chord would be G7 in 3rd inversion. When you move to the C7, your top note has to change, because there is no D in C7. Try to make it change as little as possible, making a melodic move rather than a big leap. There are two notes in C7 that are only a whole step from D (C and E). Pick either one and make that the top note of your C7 chord.

Experiment and discover for yourself what will happen when you get to the V chord, D7. You'll find that if you play the V in 1st inversion, the top voice will not have to move—the D is common to both chords (I and V).

The following example is a comping pattern in the style of guitarist Freddie King's classic shuffle, *Hideaway*. The example is in E, which is the key of the original song.

YOU CAN RUN BUT YOU CAN'T HIDE

Track 68

In *You Can Run but You Can't Hide*, the bass line is written out for your left hand. If you were on a gig with a bass player, the bass player would play that line, and you would not want to double it. Instead, you could either play nothing with your left hand, (usually a safe choice) or the root, 5, 6 shuffle pattern from page 25.

SCRATCH MY BACK COMP

In Chapter 5, you learned about playing off of triads. You can use this concept for comping as well. The following example is in the style of the comping pattern for the classic Slim Harpo tune, *Scratch My Back*. Notice the leading-tone on the third eighth note of each bar. The tension it causes makes this a very distinctive pattern.

PARALLEL 6THS

Now that you know dominant 7th chord inversions, we can change the triad pattern just a little bit to get another classic comping pattern that Jimmy Yancey favored called *parallel 6ths* (the interval between two notes in the pattern remains that of a 6th—hence the name).

Let's look again at the *Scratch My Back* pattern you learned in *The Blues Itch* and see how we can change a few things to get a parallel 6ths pattern:

Parallel Blues gives you a chance to practice the most commonly heard way of playing parallel 6ths. In this twelve-bar blues, the IV chord appears in the second bar, for just one measure. This is common in several blues styles. Next time you listen to a blues recording, listen for a "quick IV" in the second bar.

PARALLEL BLUES
Track 70

Exercise:

Transpose *Parallel Blues* into the key of D. If it seems tricky to play, start by playing a D triad and figuring out the *Scratch My Back* pattern you learned in *The Blues Itch* (page 79) in D.

80   Beginning Blues Keyboard

MINOR 7TH CHORD INVERSIONS

As you used four-note chords to comp on a dominant 7th blues, you might want to use minor 7th chords on a minor blues. This will be the case more frequently on a funky or jazz-style blues, where the harmony is specifically based on minor 7th chords.

Let's check out minor 7th chord inversions with a Cmin7 chord:

Play through the following exercise to familiarize yourself with inversions of minor 7th chords. This time we are going around the cycle of 5ths in the opposite direction, moving up in 5ths.

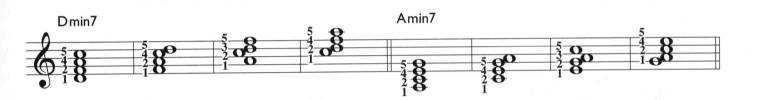

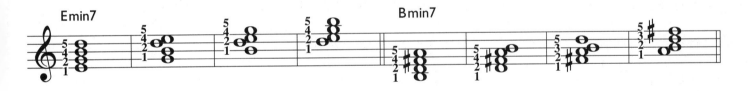

Continue up through the rest of the cycle.

The voice leading concepts you know apply when you are comping with minor 7th chords. If, for example, you wanted to start a minor blues with the root at the top of your voicing, you would use a Amin7 chord in 1st inversion:

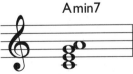

Determine which inversion of Dmin7 you would use to keep the note A as the top note of the iv chord.

Ten O'Clock Blues uses inversions of minor 7th chords. This is a funky tune with a melody, a comping pattern and a bass line pattern that introduces a new rhythm in your left hand. On the CD, you will hear the guitar playing the melody. For some help in coordinating the comping and bass parts, see the box at the bottom of the page.

TEN O'CLOCK BLUES

Track 73

To count the rhythms in each hand, subdivide each bar into eighth notes. Play each hand separately until you are comfortable with it.

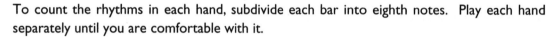

When you want to put the two parts together, make a note of which beats the hands play together and which they play apart. In this case, your two hands never play at the same time.

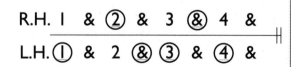

CHAPTER 8

Intros, Endings and Turnarounds

You've already got quite a blues stew going, but there are a few more essential ingredients needed. The time has come to address one of the most important and challenging aspects of blues playing—*turnarounds* and *endings*.

All those dominant 7th chords in the blues progression create continuous harmonic motion because they don't sound resolved. So, we need to have great, sometimes dramatic endings to wrap up the story. Turnarounds, on the other hand, add to the forward motion. As with any aspect of blues piano, there is a classic vocabulary to learn as well as room for your own design. We'll start with the basics.

TURNAROUNDS

A turnaround is a musical figure used to lead you back to the top of the form. A turnaround usually ends on a V7 chord (a *half cadence*) since the dominant V7 chord leads back to the tonic.

Some of the compositions earlier in this section included turnarounds. They included a V7 chord in the last bar of the form, and a repeat sign to indicate a return to the top of the form. Try to find them.

BASIC TURNAROUNDS

Bass walks up from the 3rd of the I chord to the root of the V chord.

Bass walks down from the ♭7 of the I chord to the root of the V chord.

We can put these two *chromatic* (using notes outside the key) approaches together with two hands.

The word "chromatic" also implies movement in half-step increments, as in the *chromatic scale* (a twelve-note scale which includes all of the white notes and all of the black notes on the piano).

NEIGHBORING CHORDS

To play more involved turnarounds, you need to be familiar with the neighboring chords for the key. Neighboring chords lie a half step away from the chord you are approaching. A♭7 is a neighboring chord to G7. D♭7 is a neighboring chord to C7.

Here is a basic turnaround you have already learned, but with a neighboring chord used to approach the V chord:

Play the following exercise to familiarize yourself with neighboring chords. Notice that each finger is moving only a half step. There is no need to move your hand away from the piano as you move from chord to chord. Just slide each finger to its neighboring note. Remember, all half steps on the piano are between a black note and a white note, except where the half step is between two white notes: E to F and B to C.

This exercise uses dominant 7th chords in 1st inversion. When this is mastered, try it using root position, 2nd inversion and 3rd inversion. Practice it with the left hand, too.

Example 57 is a turnaround that includes parallel 3rds in the style of Jimmy Yancey.

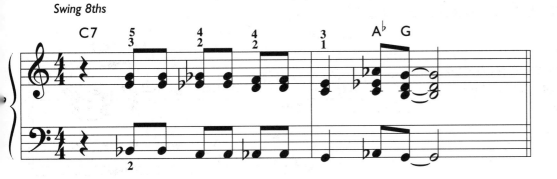

Let's take the same turnaround and make it into a triplet figure.

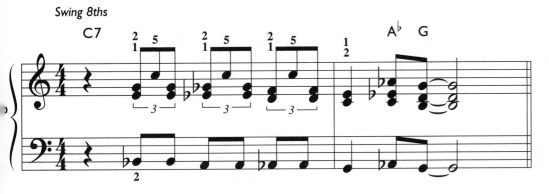

Example 59 is the "walk-up" turnaround again, but with the inner voices filled in.

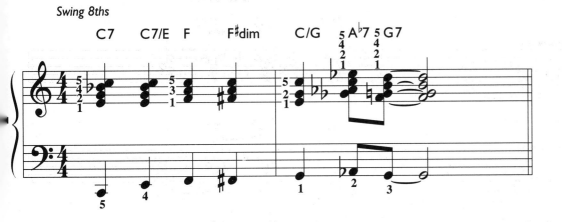

Check out the harmonic movement in this turnaround. Going from the C7 to the F is like a V7 (C7) to I (F) progression, even though this example is in C. This idea will become more important as you learn different approaches to blues playing.

Study these examples until you are comfortable enough with each turnaround to transpose it to any key.

TURNAROUND #1

TURNAROUND #2

TURNAROUND #3

Endings have the opposite function of turnarounds. Instead of taking us back to the top of the form, they take us out. Interestingly, you can transform many turnaround figures into endings just by ending on a I chord instead of the V7.

Here's a familiar turnaround transformed into an ending:

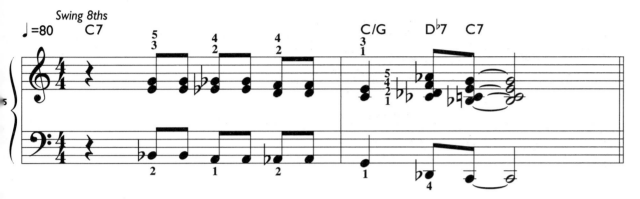

This ending approaches the I chord from below:

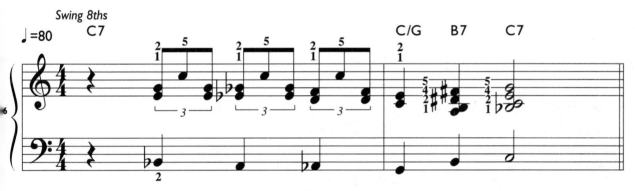

HARMONY LESSON:

Approaching a chord with its upper neighboring chord is almost the same thing as playing a V7-I7. This is because in any key, the V7 chord and the ♭II7 chord have the same 3rds and 7ths, but inverted:

In the key of C: The 3rd and 7th of G7 (V7) are B (3rd) and F (7th). The 3rd and 7th of D♭7 (♭II7) are F (3rd) and C♭, which is the enharmonic equivalent of B (7th).

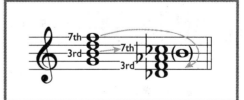

The interval between D♭ and G is called a tritone (see page 39), and **any two dominant 7th chords a tritone away from each other share the same 3rds and 7ths.**

Let's assume now that you're in a band, backing up a soloist (guitar player, singer, harmonica player, etc.). You'll need to listen and follow the soloist through the ending. He or she might want the band to *break* somewhere during the last few bars. During a break, everyone stops playing but the soloist. The soloist might play a fill in time or might play a *cadenza**. In the first case, you simply keep counting through the bars and play the last chord (or two chords ♭II7 to I7) at the right time. In the case of a cadenza, you need to stop playing and wait for the soloist's cue to come back in and end the tune.

> * A **cadenza** is an out-of-time solo passage, which can be as long or short as the soloist wishes.

Use the CD to play along with this example of a shuffle ending with a break, or try this at your next jam session.

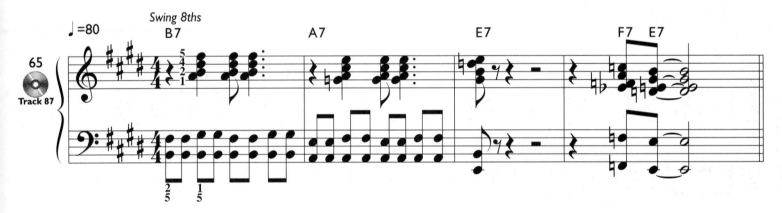

In this example, the soloist plays a cadenza on the ♭II7 and the final chord. This is shown with the *fermata* 𝄐 , or *hold* sign, over the last two chords.

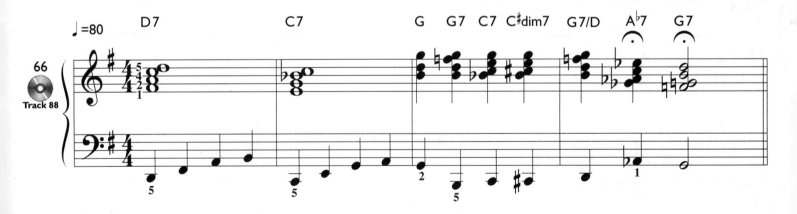

INTROS

Not every blues starts with an introduction, but many of them do. As with every other aspect of the blues that we've talked about, there is some standard vocabulary to learn, as well as some room for creativity.

A common way to start a blues is to play a four-bar, V-IV-I intro with a little turnaround at the end.

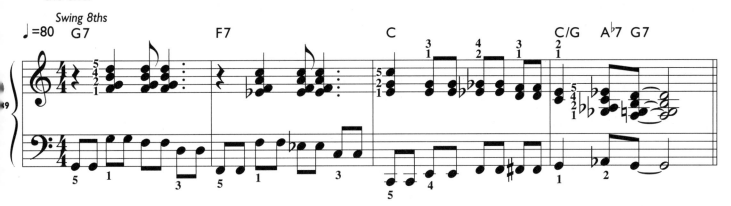

If the song you're about to play includes a riff (a short repeated figure that is the basis for the song), you or the soloist might play that riff as the intro. Notice how well the riff in bar 3 works as an intro.

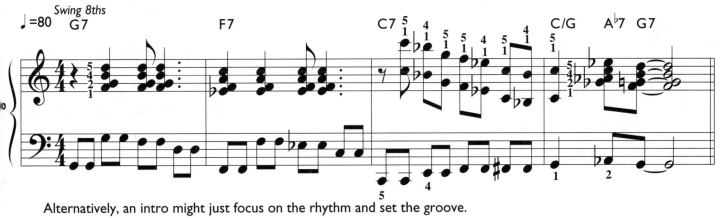

Alternatively, an intro might just focus on the rhythm and set the groove.

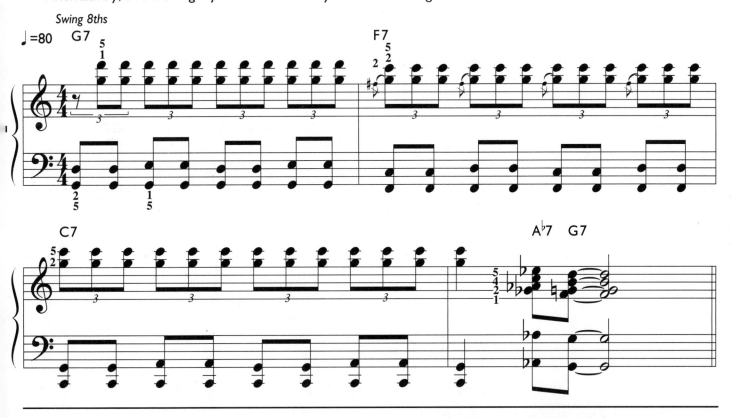

If you're playing solo piano, or you're with a band but the leader says "piano, take the intro..." then you can put any of your favorite licks or lines over the chord progression.

> **Exercise:**
>
> Pick a shuffle from earlier in the section and make up two, four-bar V-IV-I intros. Let one intro have a melodic focus, and make the other as rhythmic as possible.

Producer, composer, performer **Willie Dixon** had a career in professional boxing before pursuing a musical career. Dixon led several bands in Chicago in the 1940s. The most popular of these was The Big Three Trio, with Leonard "Baby Doo" Caston on piano—a sophisticated jump blues trio with tight arrangements by Dixon, often featuring three-part vocal harmonies. In the 1950s Willie Dixon produced sessions for Leonard Chess, wrote tunes for Chess artists like Muddy Waters, Howlin' Wolf and Little Walter and played in Muddy Waters' band. As the '50s progressed, Willie Dixon rose to greater fame and had an incredible influence on the Chicago scene. Willie Dixon claims to have written over 250 songs and has said, "I am the Blues." He certainly put his stamp firmly on blues history.

CHAPTER 9
Walking Bass and an Introduction to the Slow Blues

In Chapter 6 you were introduced to the walking bassline. In this chapter, we will look more closely at how walking lines are constructed. As a keyboard player, you are doing one of two things: either providing a bassline or responding to one. If you are not playing the bassline because there is a bass player, you need to be hearing the bass clearly enough to make good harmonic and melodic choices. A blues with a walking bassline provides many opportunities for choices because there are many different ways to "walk" through a given set of chord changes. In addition, there will be choices about which chord changes to play, especially as you start to slow down the blues, thus stretching out the progression. Playing slow blues is a huge topic which we will begin to address here, and then flesh-out further in the *Intermediate* section, where we will look at more complex chord motion, basslines and voicings, how to improvise over them and how to play in the styles of several influential blues figures.

Play *Walking the Blues* slowly, paying close attention to the left hand.

WALKING THE BLUES
Track 93

Let's look more closely at how the bassline for *Walking the Blues* is constructed:

1) Look at the first beat of each bar. In almost every measure, the root of the chord is played on the first beat. The only exceptions are bars four, eight and twelve, where the 5th of the chord is played. Notice that in each case where the 5th of the chord is played on beat one, the chord being played is the tonic I and it is being continued for a second bar. If you start your walking basslines with this kind of skeleton and fill in the blanks, you cannot go too far astray.

2) Look at the shape of the line. Most bars are either ascending (the notes all go up the staff, or descending (the notes all go down). Whether a measure is ascending or descending depends upon which octave you choose for each root when you outline the root motion. There are no hard-and-fast rules about whether you should walk up or down from one root to the next. In the first bar of *Walking the Blues*, the bass might have walked from C down to F rather than up. As always, let your ear guide you.

3) The notes you play on beats two, three and four of each bar connect the roots(or 5ths). Most of these notes come from the scale of the chord. Others are leading or *passing tones* which are outside the scale but help to connect things smoothly. Since you are walking, you will generally take small steps rather than large leaps. However, the most important thing is to make the chord changes clear and the line sound good, so there will always be some exceptions.

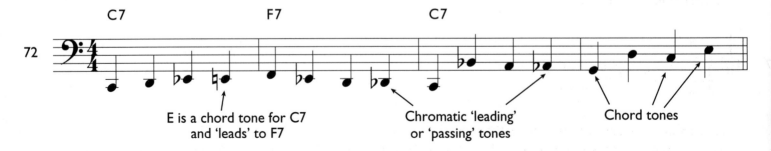

There are many ways to get from C7 (I) to F7 (IV) in four beats:

In *Walking the Blues* we walked up. We used some chromatic tones because otherwise we would have gotten to F too quickly.

An alternative might be to break up the ascending pattern, but stick to tones that are within the scale of the C7 chord (F Major).

Another way to get from C to F is to walk down.

In the twelve-bar progression, there are three times we stay on C7 for two bars. That means eight beats of C7 leading to either F7, G7 or a turnaround.

In *Walking the Blues,* we played the 5th of the chord on beat one of the second bar, but it would be OK to play the root (C) again.

You can change the direction of your walking line whenever you want. You can also put a large interval leap in wherever it seems right. The fourth bar of *Walking the Blues* doesn't walk in just one direction, but it does its job because it outlines a C7 chord and it leads to the F7 chord with the note E.

Look again at the bassline for *Walking the Blues*. This time, notice how beat four of each bar leads to beat one of the following bar. Most of the time, but not always, it will sound good to approach a root from a half-step away. Don't think of it as a rule to follow. The only rule is to make it sound good.

Chapter 9—Walking Bass and an Introduction to the Slow Blues   **93**

Here's your chance to create some bass lines. Fill in the gaps (marked with boxes) in the bass lines below. In the second example there is a melody. Make sure your bass line doesn't clash with it—stay out of its range and make sure any dissonances make sense. Let's stick to quarter notes.

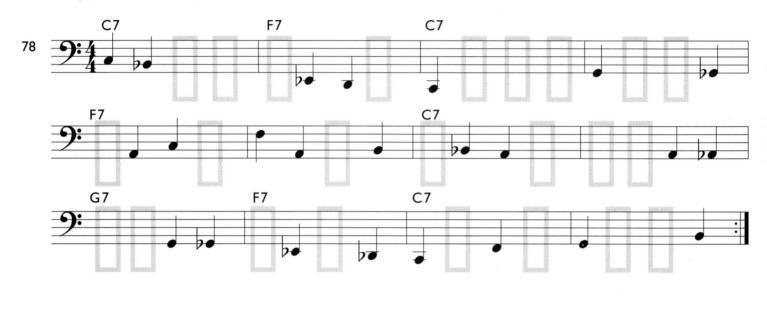

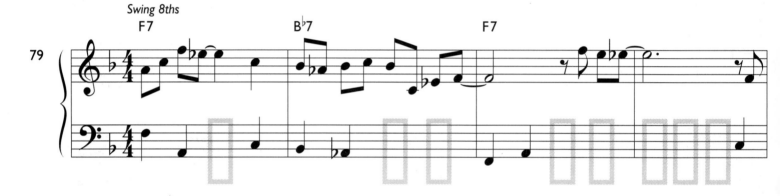

In Chapter 1, you studied diatonic triads (page 16). As you learned then, the ii chord is minor. That is why it is shown with a lower case Roman numeral. The ii-V-I chord progression is commonly used in a slow blues to substitute for the V-IV-I that normally makes up the last four bars of a twelve-bar blues. In the key of C, this progression would be Dmin7 - G7 - C.

The bass walks easily through this progression.

Sad and Lonely Blues is a slow blues in G using a ii-V-I (Amin7, D7, G7) turnaround.

SAD AND LONELY BLUES

DISCOGRAPHY

Atlantic Blues	Four-CD set including blues piano compilation with Jimmy Yancey, Professor Longhair, Meade Lux Lewis, etc. There is also great piano playing on the vocal and guitar compilations. (Atlantic Records)
Blues by Roosevelt Sykes	Roosevelt Sykes. (Smithsonian Folkways)
Blues Essentials	Compilation with Muddy Waters, Elmore James, Memphis Slim, Howlin Wolf, etc. (Capitol Records)
Birth of Soul	Ray Charles. (Atlantic Records)
Boogie Woogie, Stride and Piano Blues	With Pete Johnson, James P. Johnson, etc. (EMI Records)
Dr. John Plays Mac Rebbenack	Dr. John. (Rounder Records) Solo piano. (Clean Cuts Records)
Essential Blues Piano	Great blues piano compilation with Otis Spann, Lafayette Leake, Pinetop Perkins, Katie Webster, etc. (House of Blues)
Hoochie Coochie Man/ Got My Mojo Workin'	Jimmy Smith. (Verve Records)
Jump Back Honey	Hadda Brooks. The complete OKeh sessions (Columbia)
Live and Well Live at the Reggae	B.B. King. (MCA Records)
New Orleans Piano	Professor Longhair. (Atlantic)
Memphis Slim	Memphis Slim. (Chess MCA Records)
Patriarch of the Blues	Sunnyland Slim. (Opal Records)
Rekooperation	Al Kooper. (BMG Music)
Spiders on the Keys	James Booker (Rounder)
Texas Flood	Stevie Ray Vaughan. (Epic records). Classic example of modern blues guitar.
The Blues Never Die	Otis Spann. (Prestige Records)
The Chess 50th Anniversary Collection	Muddy Waters. (Chess/MCA Records)
The Complete Recordings	Robert Johnson. No keyboards here, but he may be the most important blues artist ever. (Columbia Records).
Vocal Accompaniment and Early Post-war Recordings: 1930-1954	Little Brother Montgomery. (Document Records)

INTERMEDIATE BLUES KEYBOARD

TRICIA WOODS

This book was acquired, edited, and produced by Workshop Arts, Inc., the publishing arm of the National Keyboard Workshop.
Nathaniel Gunod, editor
Joe Bouchard, music typesetter
Cathy Bolduc, interior design
Audio tracks recorded at Bar None Studio, Cheshire, CT

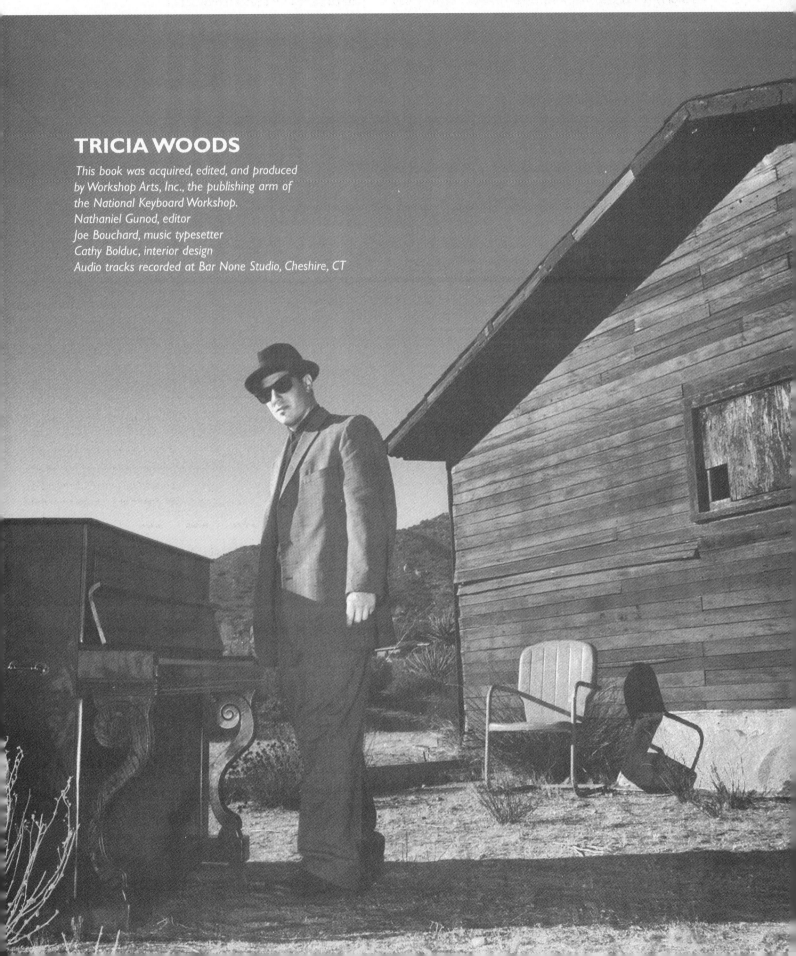

CONTENTS

INTRODUCTION

Welcome to *Intermediate Blues Keyboard*. If you have completed the first part of this book, or have started to play the blues a bit on your own already, your appetite is hopefully whet for a closer look at specific blues styles, more sophisticated harmonies and lots of grooving. One of the most satisfying aspects of studying the blues is that there is such a variety of playing styles to check out, while at the same time there are certain musical elements inherent to all blues styles. You will recognize these characteristics as a common thread running through all of the information presented here.

Expect to see repetition throughout this section. There are two reasons for this. First, and most importantly, we learn to play well through repetition. Playing the blues is not about being able to improvise using twenty different scales over one chord. It *is* about playing every chord and every note with just the right feeling. You can only achieve that by becoming very comfortable with the blues language. Secondly, the blues is folk music, passed from one player to the next. That means that as you look at a particular style, you will see new elements unique to that style as well as recurring elements common to other styles. Certain sounds and phrases that pop up in Chicago blues, for example, and again in New Orleans-style playing, even though the two styles are quite distinct.

As you progress through the *Intermediate* section, be sure to include lots of listening in your learning approach. When you listen to a recording or a live band, focus on specific elements of the music. What is the bass player doing? What is the drummer playing? Imagine yourself as the keyboard player. Expect to find yourself hearing things that you didn't notice before. This is a natural process which will occur more and more as you continue to practice, study and listen. It is a process you should be very pleased with. Look forward to having, described by another musician, "big ears." As a blues keyboard player, it's one of the highest compliments you can be paid.

Good luck, have fun, and remember "... the blues is alright."

00

Track 1

An MP3 CD is included with this book to make learning easier and more enjoyable. The symbol shown at bottom left appears next to every example in the book that features an MP3 track. Use the MP3s to ensure you're capturing the feel of the examples and interpreting the rhythms correctly. The track number below the symbol corresponds directly to the example you want to hear (example numbers are above the icon). All the track numbers are unique to each "book" within this volume, meaning every book has its own Track 1, Track 2, and so on. (For example, *Beginning Blues Keyboard* starts with Track 1, as does *Intermediate Blues Keyboard* and *Mastering Blues Keyboard*.) Track 1 will help you tune an electronic keyboard to this CD.

The disc is playable on any CD player equipped to play MP3 CDs. To access the MP3s on your computer, place the CD in your CD-ROM drive. In Windows, double-click on My Computer, then right-click on the CD icon labeled "MP3 Files" and select Explore to view the files and copy them to your hard drive. For Mac, double-click on the CD icon on your desktop labeled "MP3 Files" to view the files and copy them to your hard drive.

CHAPTER 1

Review

DIATONIC TRIADS

Diatonic means "of the key." *Diatonic triads* are triads found within the scale of a particular key.

Every major scale contains the following pattern of major, minor (min) and diminished (dim or ○) triads:

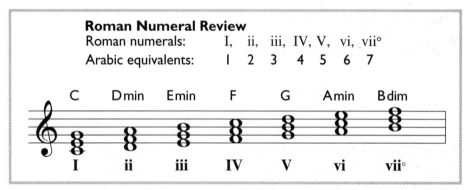

Roman Numeral Review
Roman numerals: I,   ii,   iii,   IV,   V,   vi,   vii°
Arabic equivalents: 1   2   3   4   5   6   7

We use Roman numerals to label the diatonic triads according to the degree of the scale they are built on. Upper-case numerals indicate major triads. Lower-case numerals indicate minor and diminished triads.

Let's take the key of C and build a triad on each degree of the scale using only notes found in the C Major scale.

C D E F G A B C

From the root, the notes are C, E and G—a C Major triad. This is the I chord.

From the second note of the scale, the notes are D, F and A—a D Minor triad. This is the ii chord.

Continuing up the scale we'll get:

      E Minor, iii
      F Major, IV
      G Major, V
      A Minor, vi
      B Diminished, vii°

The natural minor scale contains the following pattern of diatonic triads:

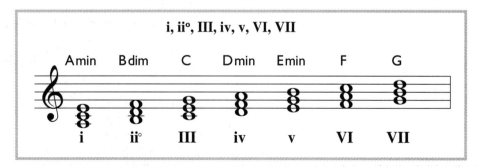

i, ii°, III, iv, v, VI, VII

FORM AND LEAD SHEETS

Measures are the building blocks of songs. The time signature, the number of measures in a song and the harmonic pattern (sequence of chords) through the measures constitutes a song's form.

In popular music, songs are often written as *lead sheets*. In a lead sheet, the melody is written but the harmony is indicated only by chord symbols over the measures.

Let's look at the following "mini-lead sheet" and describe it:

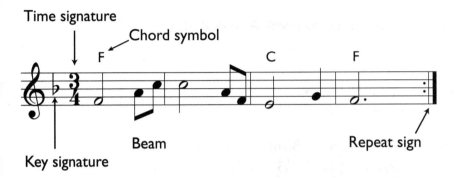

The key signature is F Major. The time signature is $\frac{3}{4}$. This means there are three beats per bar, and the quarter note gets one beat. The form is four bars long. The harmonic movement is from the I chord (F) to the V chord (C) and back. The repeat sign indicates that the form is played twice.

CYCLE OF 5THS

If we move from key to key at an interval of a perfect 5th, a sharp or flat will be added to or taken away from the key signature each time we move. This movement is called the *cycle of 5ths.* The cycle of 5ths forms the basis for most harmonic movement in our popular music.

Since an inverted perfect 5th is a perfect 4th, the cycle of 5ths is sometimes called the cycle of 4ths. It's the same thing. Usually, when blues players think "cycle of 5ths," they are thinking counter-clockwise through the cycle—down by 5ths: C, F, B♭, E♭, etc. The cycle of 5ths is also known as the *circle of 5ths.*

In this diagram, the major key cycle is on the inside. The relative minor for each major key is outside the circle. Just like the major keys, the minor keys move up in 5ths as you add sharps, and down in 5ths as you add flats to the key signature.

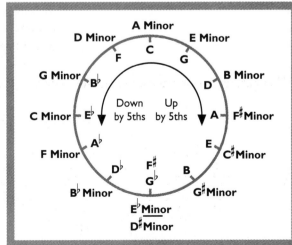

THE TWELVE-BAR BLUES

If you ask someone who loves the blues what the blues means to them, they are unlikely to start talking about chords. But if you're on the bandstand and the leader calls a "blues in G," then he is talking about chords and a specific form. It's the *twelve-bar blues*. There are a number of different blues forms, but twelve bars is by far the most common. Typically, the twelve bars are divided into three four-bar phrases. The second phrase generally repeats the first, and the third is a response to the first two. This pattern echoes the "call and response" tradition of African music which is at the root of all blues music. The three-phrase form was adopted by early blues singers who were often improvising lyrics as they sang. The harmonic structure varied somewhat, but over the years a specific chord progression emerged. This chord progression has been in use for nearly a century and is so pervasive in both blues and rock music that it is unlikely to disappear anytime soon.

The example below outlines the form of a basic twelve-bar blues. The form is twelve bars long. In other words, the harmonic pattern, or chord progression, repeats itself every twelve bars. When we improvise on blues "changes," this is the most common chord progression we play over.

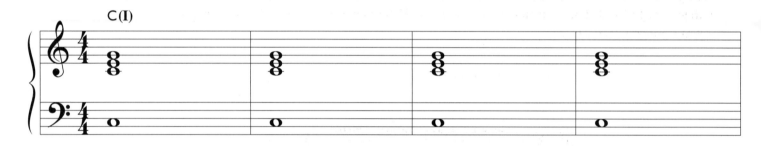

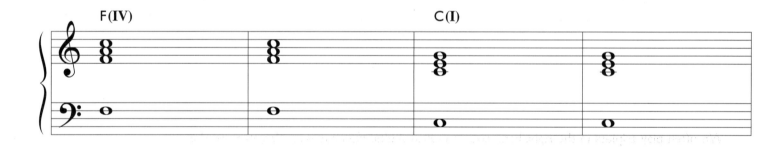

> *There are only three chords in the twelve-bar blues progression, and they are all diatonic to the key of the blues. They are the I, the IV and the V chords.*

SWING FEEL

The blues often has a $\frac{12}{8}$ feel. The time signature is still $\frac{4}{4}$, but we take each quarter note and divide it into three. In other words, we play *eighth-note triplets*. Instead of playing two eighth notes per beat, we play three. Each bar then contains twelve triplet eighth-notes, which is why it is called $\frac{12}{8}$ feel, or triplet feel. It is also often called *shuffle* feel.

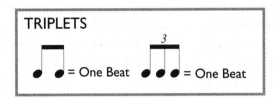

Let's get used to this feel by staying on the I chord, C Major, and playing eighth-note triplets with your right hand. Set your metronome to about 70 beats per minute and play three triplet eighth-notes on each click.

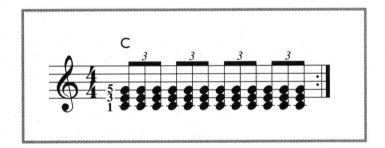

We often play triplets in the right hand over a typical shuffle bass pattern. We also use the triplet feel in the left hand, but instead of writing triplets we write eighth notes with an indication that the eighths are *swung*. *Swinging the eighths* means that the first eighth note of each beat is held longer than the second.

THE MAJOR PENTATONIC SCALE

The major and minor pentatonic scales get the name "pentatonic" from the fact that they are five-note scales. ("Penta" is the Greek word for "five." The major and natural minor scales are seven-note scales.)

Here is the "formula" for the major pentatonic scale, along with the corresponding notes in the key of C:

1	2	3	5	6
C	D	E	G	A

The scale has a major sound because the 3rd, E, is a major 3rd (four half steps above the root).

The best way to practice pentatonic scales on the keyboard is to play them with fingerings that span two octaves.

TWO-OCTAVE FINGERINGS FOR MAJOR PENTATONIC SCALES

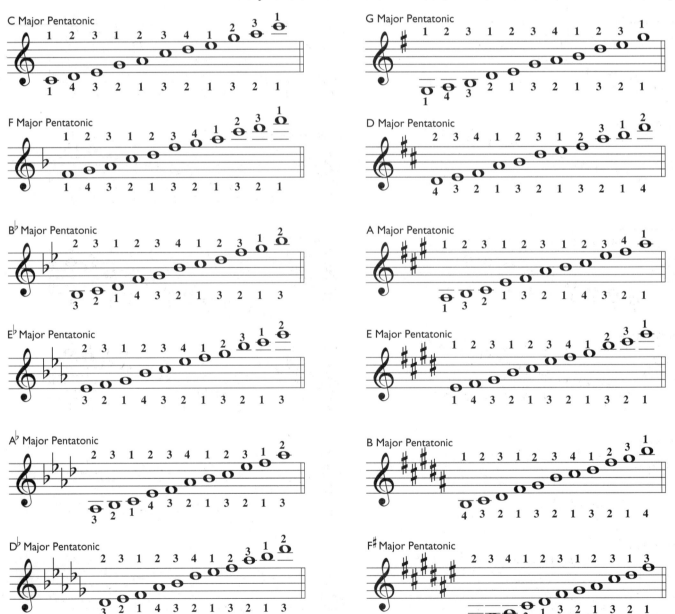

THE MINOR PENTATONIC SCALE

Just as there is a relative minor scale for every major scale, there is a relative minor pentatonic scale for every major pentatonic scale. The root of the relative minor key is a 6th above the root of the major key.

Major Pentatonic Formula:	1	2	3	5	6	1	
C Major Pentatonic:		C	D	E	G	A	(C)
A Minor Pentatonic:			A	C	D	E	G (A)

Numbering the notes of the minor pentatonic relative to its root gives us a new formula:

A	C	D	E	G
1	♭3	4	5	♭7

Let's find the notes of the C Minor Pentatonic:

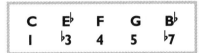

C	E♭	F	G	B♭
1	♭3	4	5	♭7

The C Minor Pentatonic scale contains two blue notes for the key of C: E♭ and B♭. It also contains chord tones from all three triads used in a C blues progression.

TWO-OCTAVE FINGERINGS FOR THE MINOR PENTATONIC SCALES

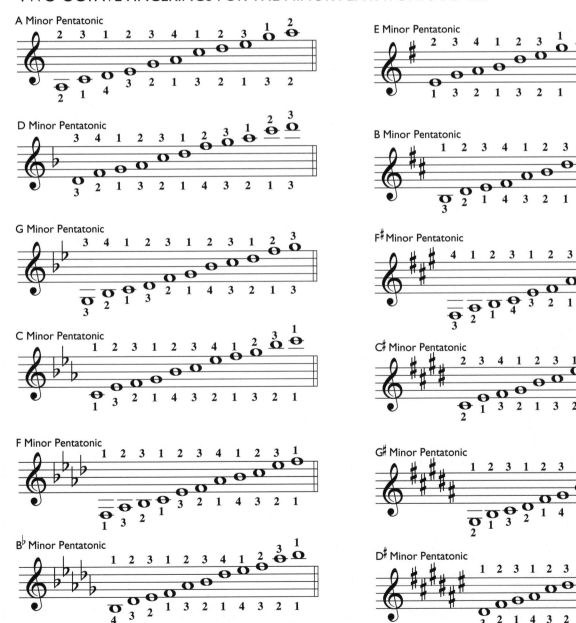

DOMINANT 7TH CHORDS

Let's look at the notes of the major scale again and this time, notice every other note:

C	D	E	F	G	A	B
1	2	3	4	5	6	7

We can use every other note of the scale to build a four-note chord:

C	E	G	B	
1	3	5	7	This is a **C Major 7** chord.

To make a C Dominant 7th chord, or **C7**, we lower the 7th by a half step (♭7), from B to B♭.

C	E	G	B♭	
1	3	5	♭7	This is a **C7** chord.

Practice playing dominant 7th chords in root position around the cycle of 5ths. Play the root of each chord in your left hand.

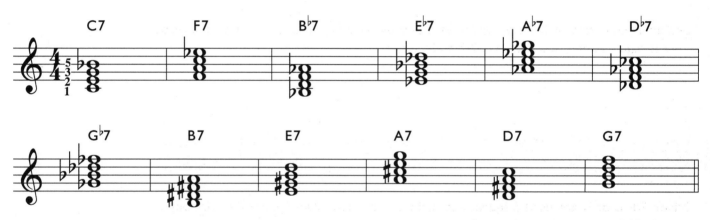

MINOR 7TH CHORDS

To make a minor 7th chord (min7), take the formula for a dominant 7th chord (1, 3, 5, ♭7) and lower the 3rd one half step (1, ♭3, 5, ♭7).

1	♭3	5	♭7
C	E♭	5	♭7

This is a Cmin7 chord.

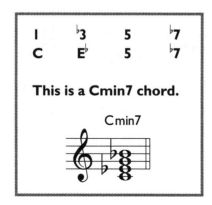

Play the dominant 7th chord exercise above, but lower the 3rd of each chord to make them all minor 7th chords.

DOMINANT 7TH CHORD INVERSIONS

Since much of blues harmony is based on the sound of dominant 7th chords, it's important to be very familiar with them in every key. You also need to be able to easily invert dominant 7th chords.

Since dominant 7th chords have four notes, they have four positions.

Let's look at a C7 chord:

Something to notice: with the exception of root position chord voicings, there will always be a whole step between the dominant 7th and the root.

MINOR 7TH CHORD INVERSIONS

Minor 7th chords are used frequently in funky or jazz-style blues, where the harmony is specifically based on minor 7th chords.

Let's check out minor 7th chord inversions with a Cmin7 chord:

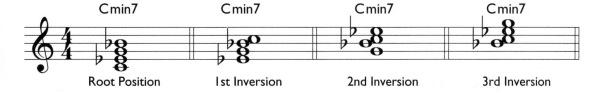

THE BLUES SCALE

We can make the minor pentatonic scale bluesier by adding one more note to it—the keyboard player's favorite blue note—the ♭5. This scale is often called *the blues scale* because it contains the notes that are considered the "blue notes" (♭3, ♭5, ♭7).

Here is the C Blues scale:

The Formula:	I	♭3	4	♭5	5	♭7
In C:	C	E♭	F	G♭	G	B♭

Since it includes all three blue notes, the ♭3, ♭5 and ♭7, this scale is going to provide you with a lot of great blues sounds. Some of your favorite licks will come out of this scale, so you should learn it very well in all twelve keys.

RIGHT-HAND FINGERINGS FOR THE BLUES SCALE IN TWELVE KEYS

Since the blues scale contains six notes, each one-octave fingering has either two groups of three (1-2-3, 1-2-3) or a group of two and a group of four (1-2,1-2-3-4).

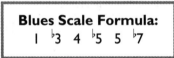

Blues Scale Formula:
I ♭3 4 ♭5 5 ♭7

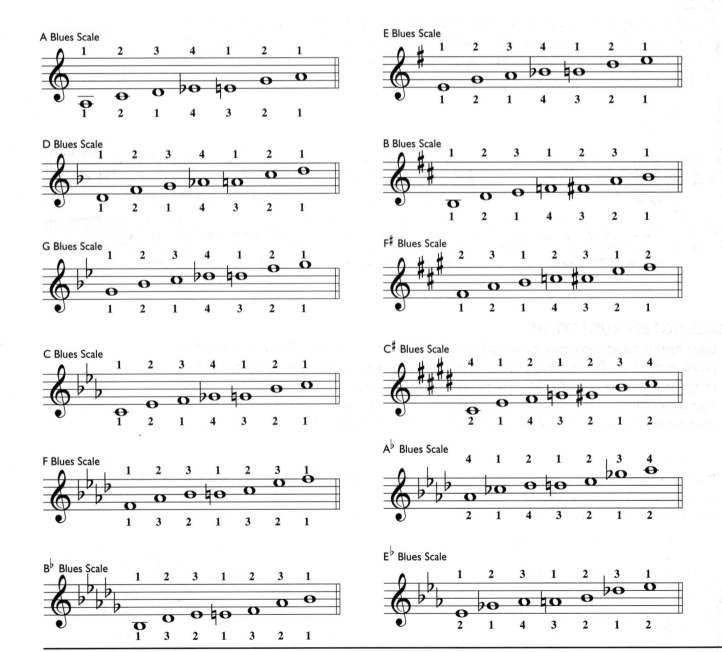

TREMOLOS

You've heard them—maybe you've already played them. If you haven't, you undoubtedly want to. *Tremolos* in the right hand, over a nice shuffle groove, are an essential ingredient in the blues sound. A trill is a rapid alternation between two notes. Sometimes blues players will call this a *roll*.

You can tremolo or roll between the root and the $\flat$3 of the key over almost the whole blues progression.

This is how trills or rolled notes are notated in the written music:

Trill on F and A$\flat$ for five beats.

Tremolos are often indicated like this:

CLUSTERS

A cluster is a group of notes that do not belong together as a chord but are played together like a chord. Often, it's just one of the notes that doesn't fit with the others. Below is an excerpt from a piece in the style of Otis Spann that was presented on page 50. The cluster (A#, B, D) is struck as a chord and then arpeggiated.

GRACE NOTES/CRUSH TONES

Grace notes are quick ornamental notes played directly before a main note. They are sometimes called *crush tones*. The $\flat$3, for example, is frequently played as a grace note preceding the 3rd in figures played off of triads. Some of us call this *bending the 3rd* because it sounds similar to a guitar player bending a note. It feels more natural in some keys than in others, depending upon where the black notes and white notes fall under your fingers. Here's how it works:

If the $\flat$3 is a black note, and the 3 is a white note, as in the keys of C, F or G, you can simply slide your 2nd finger from the $\flat$3 to the 3.

If the $\flat$3 is a white note, and the 3 is a black note, it's a little more awkward. Try playing the $\flat$3 with your 2nd finger and the 3 with your 3rd finger.

TURNAROUNDS

A *turnaround* is a musical figure used to lead you back to the top of the form. A turnaround usually ends on a V7 chord (a *half cadence*) since the dominant V7 chord leads back to the tonic.

BASIC TURNAROUNDS

Bass walks up from the 3rd of the I chord to the root of the V chord.

Bass walks down from the ♭7 of the I chord to the root of the V chord.

We can put these two *chromatic* (using notes outside the key) approaches together with two hands.

The word "chromatic" also implies movement in half-step increments, as in the *chromatic scale* (a twelve-note scale which includes all of the white notes and all of the black notes on the piano).

NEIGHBORING CHORDS

To play more involved turnarounds, you need to be familiar with the neighboring chords for the key. Neighboring chords lie a half step away from the chord being approached. A♭7 is a neighboring chord to G7. D♭7 is a neighboring chord to C7.

Here is a basic turnaround with a neighboring chord used to approach the V chord:

TURNING TURNAROUNDS INTO ENDINGS

Endings have the opposite function of turnarounds. Instead of taking us back to the top of the form, they take us out. You can transform many turnaround figures into endings just by ending on a I chord instead of the V7.

Here's a familiar turnaround transformed into an ending:

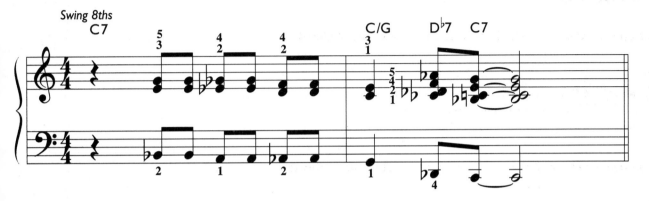

This ending approaches the I chord from below:

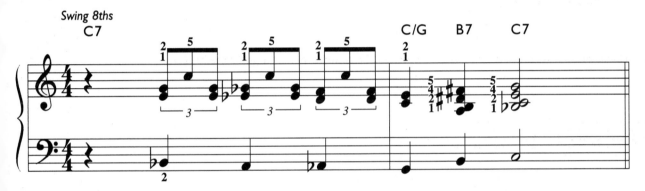

INTROS

A common way to start a blues is to play a four-bar, V-IV-I intro with a little turnaround at the end.

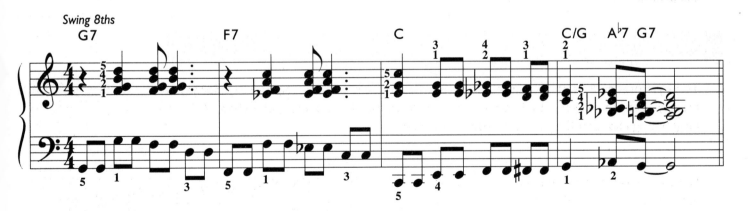

CHAPTER 2

Blues Harmony and the Eight-Bar Blues

To play the blues well, you need to know some rules but you can't follow them blindly. You always need to use your ears first.

Blues music is a fusion of African and European sounds. In this chapter, we will focus on incorporating diatonic harmony (see page 100) into your blues playing—or, more simply put—understanding and playing the key.

In the *Beginning* section of this book, we didn't concern ourselves with playing diatonic harmony. Rather, we focused on playing blues sounds. This is because all three chords in a twelve-bar blues progression are almost always dominant 7th chords (I7, IV7 and V7). Only the V7 is actually diatonic—the diatonic I and IV are major 7th chords. Since the harmonies in a blues are not strictly diatonic, one need not always think diatonically to improvise.

There is a place, however, for diatonic harmony in the blues. In fact, the peculiar combination of sometimes incorporating diatonic harmony, and sometimes bending all of its rules, is what makes the blues sound so intriguing. It is also this combination that makes learning to play the blues well an integral aspect of being a great piano player. Keep this in mind later in this chapter (starting on page 118) as you deal with information about the application of the cycle of 5ths to the blues progression.

The following exercises will reinforce your knowledge of where the major chord tones (R, 3rd, 5th and ♭7) are for each chord in a twelve-bar progression, and help your hands to learn a placement for each key. Each exercise takes you through one key. Practice each in all keys. These exercises include a classic turnaround that you should learn in every key.

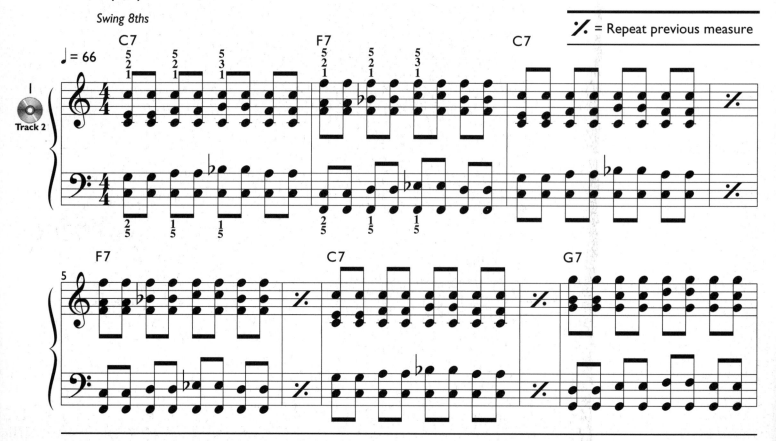

Notice that the only note your right and left hands ever *double* is the root (*doubling* is playing the same chord tone in two different octaves). The other chord tones are played only in one hand or the other, and together your two hands voice the complete chords. This is an example of playing with *open voicings*.

In **open voicings**, the voicing for each chord is spread between two hands and across more than one octave (see page 115).

The twelve-bar blues is by far the most common blues form, but there are other relatively common blues forms. Among these is the *eight-bar blues*. There are several possible chord progressions for an eight-bar blues. One of the simplest is shown below:

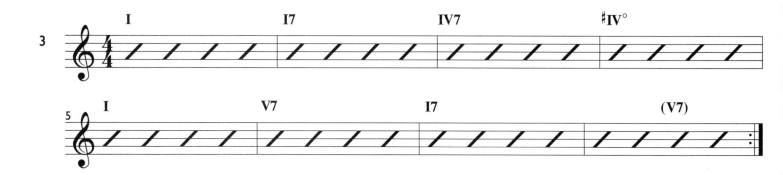

Memphis Slim taught himself to play piano as a kid and played professionally through the South before moving to Chicago in 1939. A singer and composer as well as a pianist, Memphis Slim started heading his own groups in 1946. His most well known composition was Everyday I Have the Blues. Memphis Slim was able to maintain an especially successful career through the 1950s and '60s, benefiting from a renewed interest in blues music by white Americans and a very receptive European audience. In 1963, he moved to Paris and for many years continued to perform both in Europe and the United States.

PHOTO • COURTESY OF THE INSTITUTE OF JAZZ STUDIES

Below is an eight-bar blues arranged with open voicings. With the exception of the first, fourth and fifth measures, each measure is voiced with a dominant 7th chord. Since dominant 7th chords have four notes (R, 3rd, 5th, ♭7th), we might expect to play two of those notes in one hand and the remaining two in the other. Generally, this is how open voicings work. There are, however, always exceptions.

Some chords have more notes than can be played at once, so we must choose which notes to leave out. With smaller chords, like triads, we may want to add notes and must choose what to double. Including the 5th in a chord voicing doesn't necessarily add to the sound, so we sometimes leave it out. In bar 7 of this example, the 5th is omitted and the root is doubled. The 3rd and 7th are generally not doubled (unless one of them is the melody note). Doubling 3rds and 7ths makes things sound too muddy!

Notice that the first chord, C, is voiced as a triad rather than a dominant 7th. This is characteristic of an eight bar blues; the sound of the dominant chord is emphasized in bar 2, setting up the move to the IV chord in bar 3. The I7 to IV can sound like V7 to I.

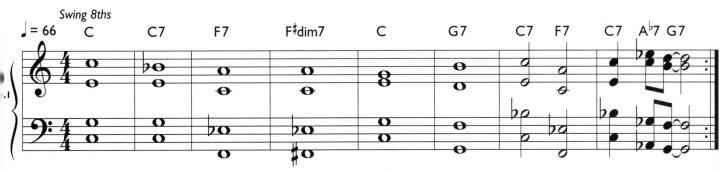

As we move forward in this book, learning about the styles and sounds of great artists like Dr. John and Ray Charles, it will become important for both of your hands to become multifunctional. Here's the same eight-bar blues arrangement with a melody added to the right hand. The right hand is now filling two roles: melody and accompaniment. Whenever possible, sustain the chord tones with the appropriate right-hand fingers while playing the melody with your remaining available fingers.

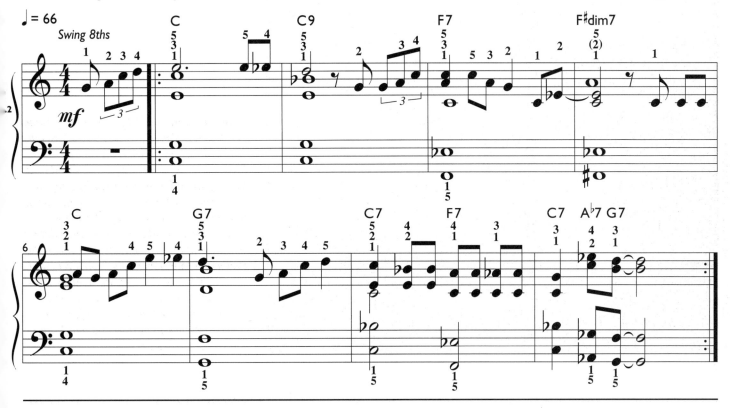

Let's take a break from harmony for a moment, and add a new sound to your blues vocabulary. Below is a classic blues piano lick that you can't live without. The Chicago blues guys used it, the New Orleans folks used it and even the jazz players use it. It works especially well on a V7-I resolution because the ♭3 moves into the major 3rd, thus highlighting the I.

Since there are two hand positions involved, it's easiest to learn it in two parts:

The first position is basically a
triad in second inversion.

The second position is based on a
triad in 1st inversion.

EXERCISE:

1) Play example 9 as shown and then continue through the cycle of 5ths. Notice that this lick is like the I-IV-I lick from page 57), except that your thumb is on the 5th rather than the root.

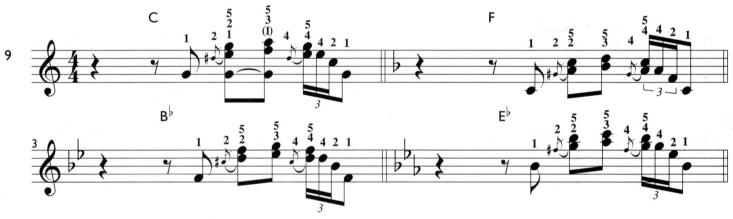

2) This is the resolving part. No doubt, you'll find yourself tagging this part of the lick onto the ends of other favorite blues sounds down the road.

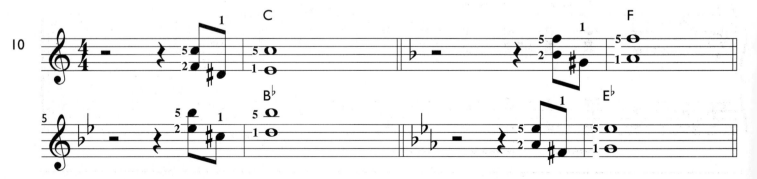

So Long is in the style of a Memphis Slim tune called *How Long?* It incorporates the resolving lick you just learned (measure 6, without the grace notes), as well as familiar sounds from the first section of this book.

SO LONG
Track 6

I-vi-ii-V HARMONY IN THE BLUES

There are times when blues changes include chords other than I, IV and V. Some progressions use more involved diatonic or cycle of 5ths harmony. This is frequently the case in a slow blues or eight-bar blues.

A full descending cycle of 5ths chord progression is as follows (see page 119 for explanation):

I	IV	iii	vi	ii	V7	I

There are songs whose chord changes include the full progression, exactly as shown above. More frequently, however, a song will:

1. Use part of the progression.
2. Move backwards and forward within the progression.
3. Involve substitutions for chords within the progression.
4. Include variations on the *chord qualities** within the progression.

A typical use of cycle of 5ths harmony within an eight-bar blues is to include I-vi-ii-V in the last four bars of the progression. Here is an eight-bar blues in the style of Memphis Slim's *Guess I'm A Fool*, arranged with open voicings:

FOOLISH BLUES
Track 7

---

* *Chord quality* refers to all the characteristics of a chord beyond its root; for example, whether it is major, minor or dominant and what *extensions* it might have. Extensions are tones beyond the 7th of a chord; 9ths, 11ths and 13ths are extensions. We'll learn more about extensions beginning on page 120.

**This is a new and interesting chord. See "variations" on next page.

HOW I-IV-iii-vi-ii-V IS DERIVED FROM THE CYCLE OF 5THS:

Starting with the I chord and moving down a 5th, we get to the IV chord. Moving down a 5th again gives us ♭VII which is not diatonic. To stay within the key, we move straight across the circle to the root a *tritone* (three whole steps) away from ♭VII which is iii, then continue downward in 5ths to get vi, ii, V and I.

VARIATIONS

You encountered yet another new chord in bar 4 of *Foolish Blues*: the D♭7, which is the ♭VII of the key (E♭). Some might also call it the *IV of IV* because relative to the IV chord (A♭7), D♭7 is the IV chord.

Putting the ♭VII, or IV of IV in bar 4 of an eight-bar blues is a common variation on this progression. Another example of this is Willie Nelson's *The Night Life Ain't No Good Life*. Other variations occur, especially in the last two bars or turnaround section (see page 110) of the progression.

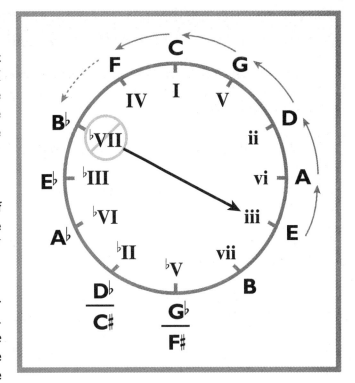

The following chart shows some of the harmonic possibilities for an eight-bar blues progression:

Eight-Bar Blues Harmonic Possibilities

Measure:	1	2	3	4	5	6	7	8
Possible Harmonies:	I7	I7	IV7	iv* - ♭VII7	III7 - VI7	II7 - V7	III7 - VI7	II7 - V7
		I		♭VII7	iii - VI7	ii - V7	iii - vi	ii - V7
				♯IV°	I7 - vi	V7	IV7	V7
				IV7	I		I7 - IV7	I7 - V7

*Remember, upper case Roman numerals indicate major or dominant harmonies. Lower case Roman numerals indicate minor or diminished harmonies.

So far, we have been looking at chords with four or less different notes. We can add more notes to our chords. The extra notes are called *extensions*. Extensions on a chord do not change the chord's *function* (the way it acts in a progression), but they do change its color.

Remember, we build chords in 3rds (using every other note of a scale). Following the 7th, the next chord tone is the 9th. The chart below shows the chord tones and the extensions beyond the 7th. For convenience, we'll relate it to a C root.

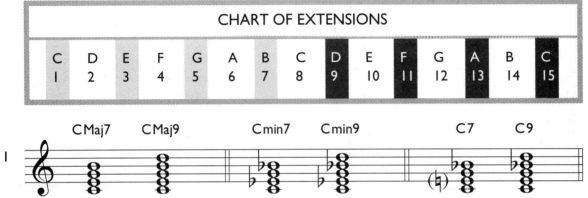

■ = Chord tones

■ = Extensions

Notice that the extensions are simply the notes of the scale in the next octave. For example, the 9th is the 2nd in the next octave. Extensions give us more possibilities for voice leading because we have more notes from which to choose. We must use extensions with care, otherwise they will detract from, rather than add something to, the music. Blues keyboardists frequently use 9ths as the top voice of their chords.

Continuing up the scale past the 9th, we reach the 11th and the 13th. These are common extensions, but not on all types of chords. The 11th, for instance, doesn't sound good on a major or dominant 7th chord because it clashes with the major 3rd (it is, after all, just the 4th up one octave). It sounds fine, however, on a minor chord. The 13th is used most frequently on dominant 7th chords.

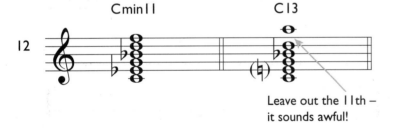

Leave out the 11th –
it sounds awful!

On dominant chords, extensions may be altered by raising or lowering them a half step. The correct way to notate a chord with an altered extension is to list the altered extension separately from the rest of the chord, placing a comma before it. Extensions are always listed from the lowest to the highest.

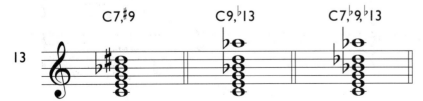

Let's look at *Foolish Blues* again, this time with the piano part arranged as an accompaniment behind a solo instrument (voice, guitar, etc.). Notice how chord extensions are used in the voice leading—the top notes of each chord combine to make a simple melody.

Track 8

FOOLISH BLUES #2

CHAPTER 3

Improvising in a Blues Style

The blues is improvised music. Most blues keyboard music is not written down. It is up to you to create it. Learning to work within certain harmonic and stylistic parameters specific to the blues and studying the styles of great players builds a foundation from which to work on improvising. In this chapter, we'll focus on adding more vocabulary to your blues language and developing the improvising techniques you need to create your own voice.

MORE RESOLVING LICKS

As an improvising musician, you may have an aversion to "licks." You might think that playing licks is not really improvising, and that developing "ideas" is what it's all about. You need both in the blues. Blues is folk music. The blues tradition was passed from generation to generation as younger musicians listened to and emulated older musicians. The music has evolved and developed tremendously, but the sounds that said "I've got the blues" in 1945 still say that today. To be a convincing blues player, you need to learn these sounds. They are the "words" of your "language." Just as when you speak you compose your own sentences, so when you play the blues you'll be putting sounds together in your own way.

Examples 14, 15 and 16 contain licks (in the grey boxes) that will take you back to the I chord at the end of a phrase or chorus. Each lick is played in the context of the last four bars of a twelve-bar blues (V, IV, I).

The lick in example 14, in the style of Hadda Brooks, is a variation on the lick you learned in Chapter 2. Most of the notes are from the major pentatonic scale. In the last beat of measure three, notice how the major 3rd of the I chord is approached by the two leading tones—one a half-step above, and one a half-step below. This is probably the most traditional and common way of resolving a blues or jazz line to the I chord.

This lick, in the style of Roosevelt Sykes, is based on a combination of the minor and major pentatonic scales. The major 3rd is never played, making this a perfect sound to use on blues tunes which are not strongly major or minor (where the harmony consists mainly of roots, 5ths and 6ths, thus leaving the 3rd undefined).

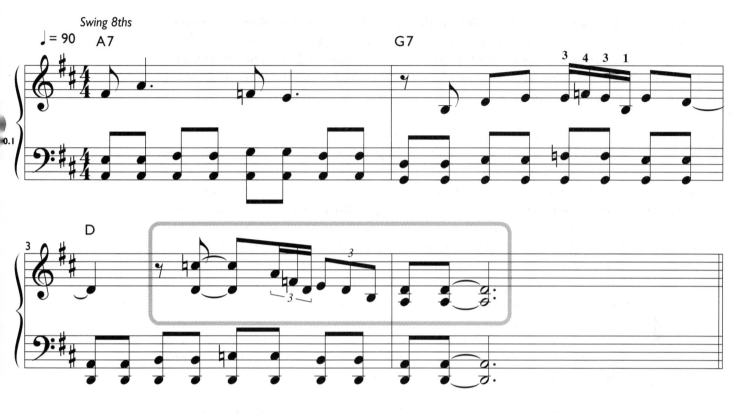

Below is another lick resolving to a major I, this time in the style of Memphis Slim. Check out how the rhythm at the end of the first phrase sets up the repetition of the phrase an octave lower. Blues pianists commonly extended their phrases this way. There is repetition involved, but it flows like one big sentence.

PLAYING DIATONIC LINES

In the *Beginning* section, we discussed blues melodies and how to create them. We talked about playing the major and minor pentatonic scales or a combination of both. Piano players most frequently play a combination. This is because our instrument is generally filling multiple roles simultaneously (melodic, harmonic and rhythmic). Remember, since the blues sound includes the tension of dominant harmonies against blue notes, your improvising needs to include both.

Recall that if we combine major and minor pentatonic scales, we have all but one of the chord tones (the 3rd of the V chord is not included) from the I-IV-V progression of a twelve-bar blues (see page 40). If we add 9ths to the dominant chords (the note D for C9, G for F9 and A for G9), we are still playing notes from the combined pentatonic scales for the key of C. So, we can build elegant melodic lines off of the chord structure. Play along with the CD, letting your left hand rest while the bass player walks a line for you. Otherwise, add a simple shuffle pattern with your left hand.

Passing tones are included in several places to make the melody smoother. Notice how they occur on off-beats (the second of a pair of eighth notes) and connect two diatonic tones.

IT'S A FINE LINE

Jay "Hootie" McShann (*James Columbus McShann*) *came out of the Kansas City blues scene of the 1930s. He led several successful "jump blues" bands, including one band featuring the young Charlie Parker on alto saxophone. Jay McShann plays in a clean, elegant, jazz-influenced blues style with an emphasis on line. After years of refining his vocal accompaniment techniques, he developed his own vocal skills to become a successful blues singer as well as pianist.*

PHOTO • BILL WEILBACHER

DIATONIC LINES THROUGH ARPEGGIOS

Practice playing dominant chord arpeggios by inserting them into little musical phrases.

An alternative to playing licks or outlining chords is to use a *motif* (a short melodic or rhythmic figure that repeats) as the basis for your solo. A motif as short as three or four notes can be the basis of a great solo if it is carefully developed.

Let's start with this motif in C.

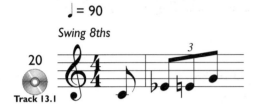

Let's look at a solo now, four bars at a time. The motif is stated in bar 1, repeated in bar 2, repeated again with an extra note in bar 3 and, for variety, repeated starting on a different beat of the bar with an extra note in bars 3 and 4.

Bars 1-4:

The motif has to be altered to fit the F7 chord in bar 5, then it's repeated in bar 6, repeated minus its first note and with an E natural in bar 7 and repeated with a new note inserted (A) in bars 7 and 8. This creates a new idea, which is then repeated.

Bars 5-8:

Like a balloon, the idea is inflated a little bit more in bar 9 with the addition of the A and C afterward and finally is integrated into a typical ending phrase.

Bars 9-12:

RHYTHMIC VARIATION

We varied the motif in the preceding example by shifting its position within the bar. Another means of changing it rhythmically is to change the rhythmic value of the notes.

For example:

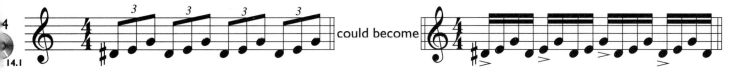

The new version sounds quite different because the placement of the motif against the on-beats (those your ear hears most strongly because they fall on the beat) keeps changing.

You might also change the rhythmic density of an idea by starting with space in the idea, and then making the idea more rhythmically dense. This is sometimes called *diminution*.

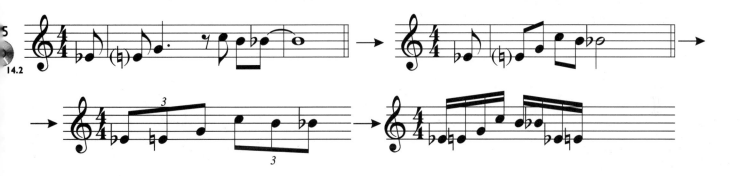

Leaving space at the beginning of a blues solo as demonstrated in example 25 is important for two reasons:

1. It gives the listener time to absorb your ideas.
2. It gives you room to develop your story.

Every good story has a beginning, a climax and an ending. Keeping this in mind, begin your solo at a reasonable pace and it will remain interesting as it unfolds. The *Mastering* section explores additional methods of developing an extended solo.

Exercises:

1. Choose any key and write a three- or four-note motif. Play it starting on three different rhythmic points within the bar. It can start on an on-beat or an off-beat.

2. Choose another key, and write a short motif which contains space. Compress it (less space, shorter note values) at least twice.

HARMONIZING LINES IN 6THS AND 3RDS

On page 68, you played a tune in the style of Jimmy Yancey using parallel 3rds and on page 79 you learned a parallel 6ths comp. In both cases, you were playing *dyads* (two notes played at once). Playing simple melodic lines as dyads is a very effective way of making them sound great and is a technique used extensively in blues piano.

PARALLEL 6THS

When you harmonize a melody in 6ths, use major or minor 6ths as necessary to fit the chord you are playing over.

Below is an exercise in playing 6ths through a blues progression. Passing tones are used on weak beats (beats 2 and 4) where necessary to allow resolved sounds (chord tones) to fall on strong beats (1 and 3). Play a basic comp in the left hand.

Simple motifs can be harmonized in 6ths. Again, we must adjust the qualities as necessary to fit the chords. Example 27 shows the same motif over I (C7) and IV (F7).

PARALLEL 3RDS

As you know, every interval can be inverted (turned upside down). For example, the interval from C up to A, a major 6th, can be inverted to A up to C (a minor 3rd). Notice that $6 + 3 = 9$; interval + inversion always equals 9. Notice also that when inverted, a major interval always becomes minor, and vice versa. The inversion of a major 6th is a minor 3rd; the inversion of a minor 6th is a major 3rd. Playing lines harmonized in 3rds is similar to 6ths, but has a "closer" sound. Check out this comparison:

September Blues uses a combination of 3rds and 6ths and lots of passing tones!

SEPTEMBER BLUES

Track 17

When you improvise, you'll use a combination of the various tools at your disposal. Your solo should contain ideas of your own, as well as the occasional perfectly placed classic lick to pull things together. Your playing on the gig should be as spontaneous as possible. Avoid giving a whole lot of deliberate thought to what elements you want to include in your solo. If you're busy thinking, you are not "in the moment." At home, however, it's great to practice putting different ideas together to see what works.

Try combining two or more approaches in one line, using newer concepts from this section and your old workhorses from the *Beginning* section. For example:

Three-Note Motif and Descending 6ths

Repeated Blues Scale Cluster and Parallel 3rds Leading to Resolving Lick

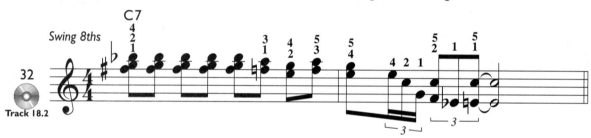

Classic ♭5 Blues Lick Combined with Playing Off of a Dominant Chord

Outlining the Chords Followed by a Descending Minor Pentatonic Scale

On the next page there is a two chorus solo in G, illustrating many of the techniques and concepts we've covered. The left hand is not written; choose a simple shuffle pattern and add it yourself. Play through the solo quite slowly, then try to pick out examples of the different licks and sounds you've been working on. Don't let the appearance of a lot of notes throw you. Remember, the object is for you to create your own solos. You won't be reading pages like this if you're playing the blues. That's why it's important for you to understand and *hear* what you're playing.

DOIN' IT

Track 19

$\boxed{\overset{3}{\bullet\ \bullet\ \bullet}}$ = A quarter-note triplet. Three equal notes in the time of two beats.

Exercises:

1. Play a simple left-hand shuffle pattern in G at a comfortable tempo, and improvise two twelve-bar choruses over it. Focus on keeping the left hand steady, and don't be afraid to leave space in your solo.

2. Compose two twelve-bar choruses over the same shuffle pattern. Write them out, memorize them and learn to play them smoothly.

CHAPTER 4

Focus on the Left Hand

Of all keyboard styles, the blues might be the most focused on the left-hand. As the blues evolved, guitarists actually copied left-hand piano parts because they propelled the music so effectively. When you are playing solo piano, your left hand is your band and, literally, can't miss a beat. To be able to play rock-solid at any tempo, you need to pay some special attention to your left hand.

REVIEW

Following is a review of the left-hand parts covered in the first two sections of this book.

SHUFFLES
Swing the 8ths in all of them!

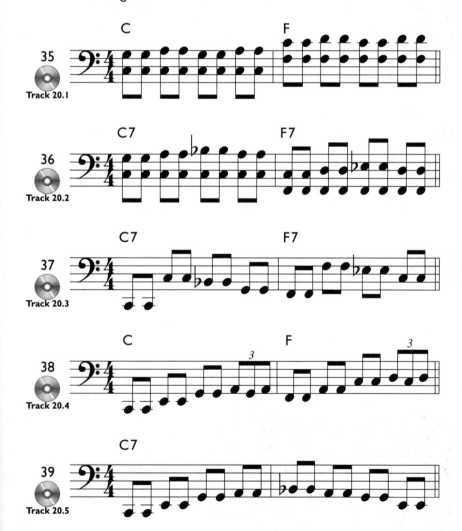

WALKING BASS

FUNKY (STRAIGHT EIGHTHS)

BOOGIE-WOOGIE
Swing the 8ths.

AS PART OF CHORD VOICINGS

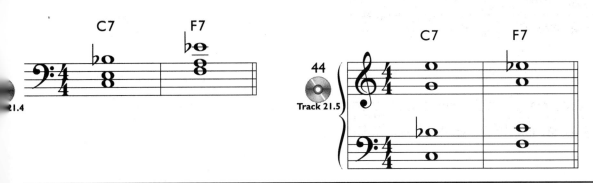

WALKING BASS LINES

Once you understand the fundamentals of building a walking bass line (see page 91), the next step is to develop your vocabulary. Knowing that there is more than one way to get from the I chord to the IV chord is one thing, but having it under your fingers is another. You need to practice different ways of getting through chord progressions so you don't always play exactly the same thing. As always, the best way to discover new sounds is by listening to recordings and transcribing what you hear. Here are some typical walking patterns to get you started.

SIX WAYS TO GET TO THE IV CHORD ON THE DOWNBEAT OF BAR 2

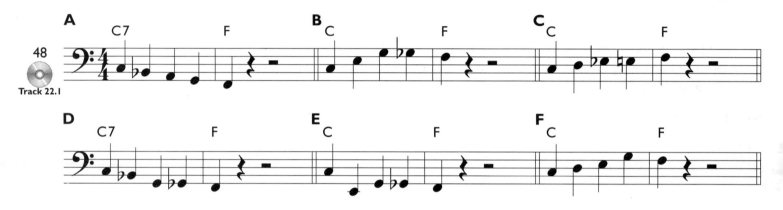

FOUR ROUTES BACK TO I

These assume we used example 48A get to the IV chord. Similar solutions will work for 48B-F.

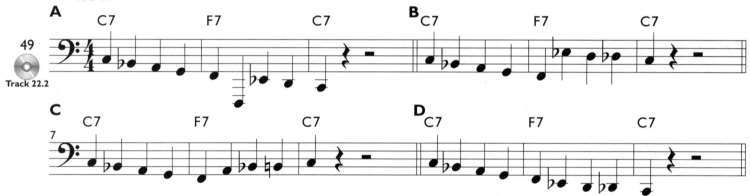

FOUR WAYS TO STAY ON I FOR EIGHT BEATS

Sometimes it seems tricky to stay on one chord for several bars. Any two of these two-bar ideas can be combined to fill four bars.

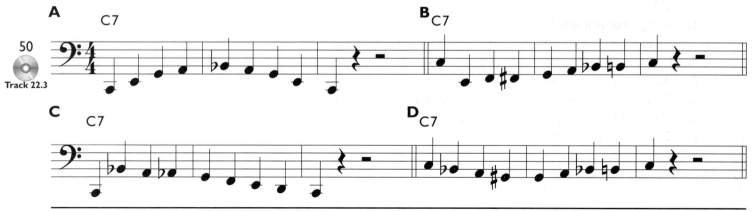

FOUR WAYS TO WALK THROUGH I-vi-ii-V

In Chapter 2, you played an eight-bar blues on page 118 called *Foolish Blues*. Here are two choruses of walking through the same blues progression. Recall the melody of *Foolish Blues* and add it in your right hand.

Top Ten Tips for Walking Bass Lines

1. Play the root on beat one of the bar frequently. The 5th can work, too, or in the proper context, another chord tone such as the ♭7.
2. Think ahead—know where you are going.
3. Play primarily diatonic tones on the strong beats of the bar (beats 1 and 3). Reserve leading tones, passing tones or chromatic tones for the weak beats (beats 2 and 4).
4. Repeat notes (especially the root) if you wish.
5. Add occasional eighth notes if they make the line flow more smoothly.
6. Combine measures of walking with other typical bass patterns (boogie, shuffle, etc.).
7. Think of the bass line as a second melody.
8. Sing a bass line, then play it.
9. Vary your lines with octaves.
10. Keep it simple.

ROOTS, 3RDS, 7THS AND 10THS

In most cases, the root, 3rd and 7th of a chord define a chord's function and quality. In some blues styles, you can play solely a combination of roots, 3rds and 7ths for your left-hand accompaniment. It's necessary to be very familiar with the locations of the 3rds and 7ths in every key so you can use them easily for your blues progressions.

If you are playing with a bass player, you can play just the 3rd and 7th of each chord.

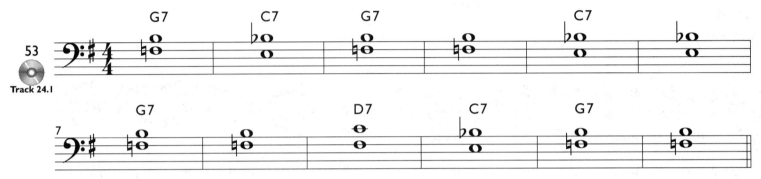

When playing solo, alternate between the root-7th and root-3rd.

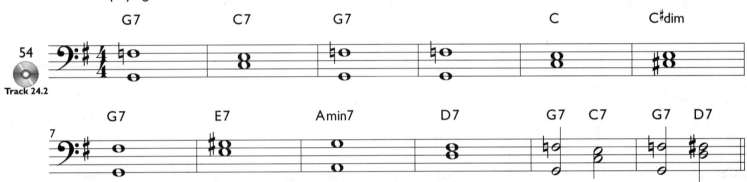

If your hand is big enough, you can play 10ths, one of the nicest sounds on the piano. A 10th is simply a 3rd with an extra octave inserted, giving it a more open sound. If you can't reach a 10th, fake it by rolling your hand quickly from the bottom note to the top note.

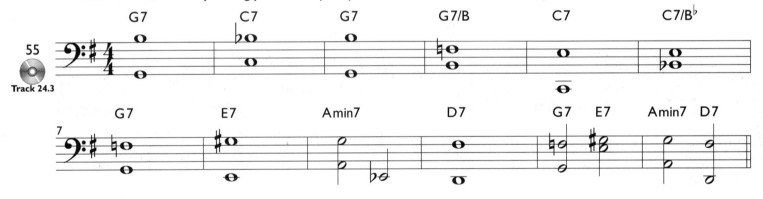

For a fuller sound, combine some walking lines with 3rds, 7ths and 10ths.

136   Intermediate Blues Keyboard

Some of the hottest players walk 10ths. *Blues for Lefty* is based on the classic blues *C. C. Rider.*
Try playing it slowly, keeping your left hand as relaxed as possible. Learn the left hand alone,
first. If the 10ths feel like too much of a stretch, roll them or skip this for now and come back
to it when you're ready. Some people with small hands never feel comfortable with 10ths.
It's okay! We have lots of other tools at our disposal.

BLUES FOR LEFTY

* Tremolo the thumb with the upper three fingers.

LEFT-HAND COMBINATIONS

Now that you have acquired so much left-hand vocabulary, you can custom-design your bass lines by combining different patterns and ideas. For example:

COMBINE A WALK UP WITH A SHUFFLE PATTERN

The *walk up* is in bar 4.

57 Track 26.1

WALK THEN SHUFFLE

58 Track 26.2

WALK BOOGIE-WOOGIE STYLE

59 Track 26.3

WEAVE A MELODIC IDEA INTO YOUR LEFT-HAND PART

60 Track 26.4

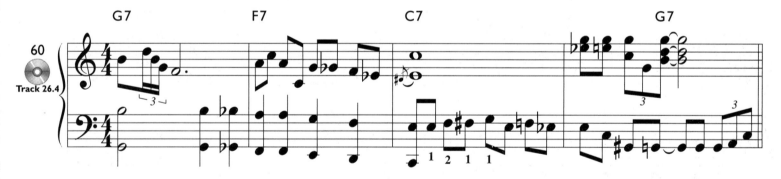

DOUBLE THE RIGHT AND LEFT HANDS FOR DRAMATIC EFFECT

61 Track 26.5

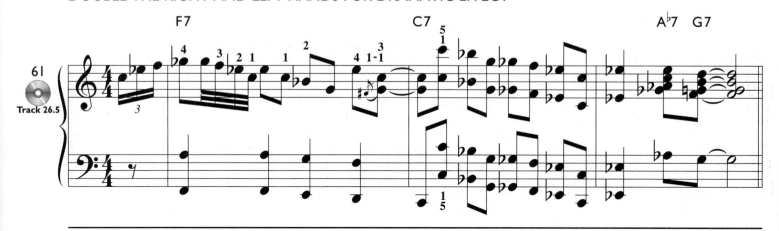

This tune is a great example of different types of bass lines combined for a varied effect.

SCHIZOPHRENIC BLUES

Track 27

♩ = 90

Swing 8ths

Jelly Roll Morton *called himself the inventor of jazz. He took the music of his day, ragtime and blues, and added new sounds, opening it up to new ways of improvising and setting it in sophisticated arrangements. Like the music around him, Jelly Roll was of mixed African and European descent. Between 1917 and 1940, Morton played and recorded in New Orleans, Los Angeles, Chicago and New York. His own band, the Red Hot Peppers, gave Victor Records its first hits in 1926 and 1927. Several of Morton's best known compositions, like* King Porter Stomp *and* Chicago Breakdown *became favorites of other major bands of the 1920s and '30s, and were recorded by artists like King Oliver and his Creole Jazz Band, Fletcher Henderson and Glenn Miller.*

STRIDE PIANO

Jelly Roll Morton and James P. Johnson (about whom you'll learn more in the *Mastering* section) both played stride piano. In stride piano, the left hand plays an alternating root-chord pattern. Generally roots, which might be played in octaves, are played on beat 1, roots or other chord tones are played on beat 3, and triads or simple chord voicings are played on beats 2 and 4.

Track 28.1

The bass line within the stride pattern should be interesting and provide forward motion. Frequently, as in example 63, it will incorporate bits of walking.

Track 28.2

A richer sound is achieved by alternating 10ths with interesting chord voicings. It also helps to include bars of walking 10ths. If the stretch is too hard, roll the 10ths or skip this example.

Track 28.3

Stride by Stride is an example of stride left hand on a twelve-bar blues.

STRIDE BY STRIDE

Track 29

Exercises:

Write out a stride pattern through a twelve-bar or eight-bar blues progression of your choosing. Use your ears and your understanding of walking bass lines to keep the bass movement interesting. Include at least one bar which walks. Memorize the pattern and learn to play it smoothly in two different keys.

CHAPTER 5

More Harmony/Slow Blues

In Chapter 2, you learned about chord extensions and using different chord progressions in the blues. We also talked about more complex harmonic movement. This chapter will continue to explore those areas by looking at more advanced harmonies and applying them to two classic slow blues progressions.

HARMONY OVERVIEW: TRIADS, 7TH CHORDS, EXTENSIONS, ALTERED EXTENSIONS AND SUS CHORDS

Let's begin with a chord review.

Triads are the foundation for more complex chords. There are four types of triads:

TRIADS

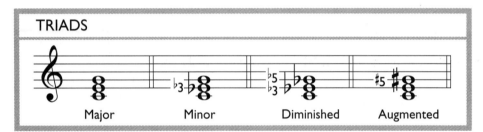

Major Minor Diminished Augmented

Augmented triads are not diatonic to either the major or minor scales. They have a very unresolved sound and, for this reason, the chord most frequently augmented is the V chord. We will see an example of this shortly.

Major or minor 7ths may be added to all four types of triads, resulting in the chord-types shown in the chart below.

7TH CHORD-TYPES

Chord-Type	Formula	Example in C	Chord Notation
Major 7	1,3,5,7	C,E,G,B	CMaj7; C△7; CM7
Dominant 7	1,3,5,♭7	C,E,G,B♭	C7
Minor 7	1,♭3,5,♭7	C,E♭,G,B♭	Cmin7; C-7; Cm7
Minor/major7	1,♭3,5,7	C,E♭,G,B	Cmin/maj7; C-maj7
Minor 7,♭5 or half diminished	1,♭3,♭5,♭7	C,E♭,G♭,B♭	Cmin7,♭5; C7,♭5; Cø
Diminished	1,♭3,♭5,6	C,E♭,G♭,A	C°
Major 7,♯5 (augmented)	1,3,♯5,7	C,E,G♯,B	CMaj7,♯5; CMaj7,+5
Augmented dominant	1,3,♯5,♭7	C,E,G♯,B♭	C7Aug; C+5

In addition to 7ths, we can add extensions—9ths, 11ths and 13ths—to most chords.

EXTENSIONS

Chord type	Common Extensions	Extensions in C
Major	9, ♯11, 13	D, F♯, A
Minor	9, 11	D, F
Dominant	9, ♯11, 13	D, F♯, A

On major and dominant chords, the 11th is a $^\sharp$11 to avoid making the interval of $^\flat$9 (a very *dissonant*, clashing sound) between the major 3rd and the natural 11th.

Dominant chords frequently have altered extensions and/or altered 5ths. Chord extensions and alterations are used in the blues for color, to add a dimension of tension and release, and to create interesting melodic voice leading.

ALTERED EXTENSIONS	
Chord (with C roots)	**Notes**
C7,$^\flat$9	C,E,G,B$^\flat$,D$^\flat$
C7,$^\sharp$9	C,E,G,B$^\flat$,D$^\sharp$
C7,$^\flat$9,$^\sharp$5 or C7,$^\flat$9,+5 or C7Alt *	C,E,G$^\sharp$,B$^\flat$,D$^\flat$
C7,$^\sharp$9,$^\sharp$5 or C7+9,+5 or C7Alt *	C,E,G$^\sharp$,B$^\flat$,D$^\sharp$
C13,$^\flat$9	C,E,G,B$^\flat$,D$^\flat$,A
C13, $^\sharp$9	C,E,G,B$^\flat$,D$^\sharp$,A
C9,$^\flat$5	C,E,G$^\flat$,B$^\flat$,D
C9,$^\flat$13** (or C9,$^\sharp$5)	C,E,G$^\sharp$,B$^\flat$,D

* These chords are both called *altered chords* (Alt). An altered chord has neither a natural 5th nor a natural 9th.

** In a chord with a $^\flat$13, omit the natural 5th to avoid creating a $^\flat$9 interval within the chord.

SUS CHORDS
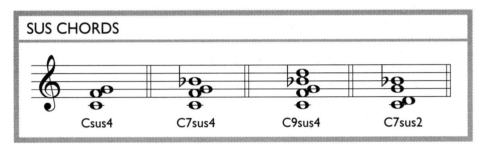

Another type of chord used frequently in blues, gospel and rock music, is the *suspended chord* (sus). Sus chords have one of their chord tones (usually the 3rd), raised or lowered. The most common sus chords are the sus4, in which the 3rd is raised to become a 4th, and the sus2, in which the 3rd is lowered to become a 2nd.

In slow blues progressions, the V chord is sometimes played as a sus4. Take a look at how this is applied in a ii-V-I chord progression. With the exception of the note G, all of the notes from G9sus4 are found in Dmin7. So, in example 65, the voicing in the right hand can stay the same when switching between those two harmonies.

An altered V chord is commonly voiced with the #5 or the root as the top note. Practice both of these voicings through the cycle of 5ths. Examples 66 and 67 will get you started with each.

3RD INVERSION (#5 ON TOP)

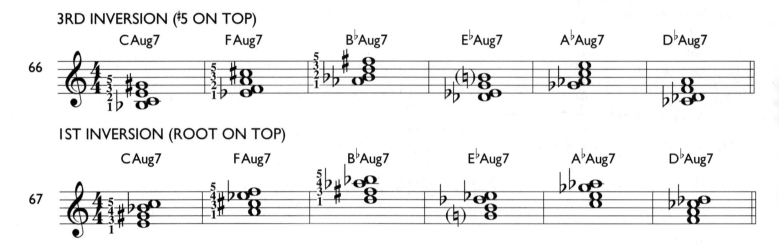

1ST INVERSION (ROOT ON TOP)

The I chord often includes a natural 13th. We think of it as a 13th rather than a 6th because the ♭7 is present. The 13th chord sounds great preceded by a neighboring chord (the same chord, one half step higher).

It is important to learn the two inversions of a sus4 chord. Example 69 has three ii-V-I progressions. The V chords are all sus4 chords. The right hand plays them in two inversions: 1st inversion (the 4th replaces the 3rd on the bottom) and 2nd inversion. Since the left hand holds the root through the V measures, the true position of all the sus4 chords in this example is root position.

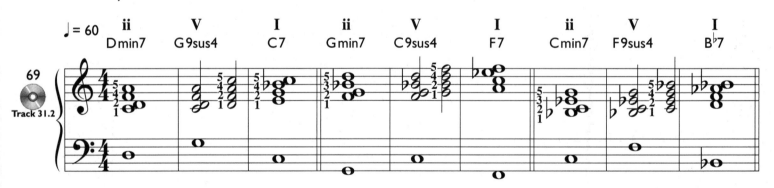

To get the most out of these examples, and all others like them, try to learn them in all twelve keys. While you don't have to do this in one sitting at first, it's an important thing to do. You need to learn to play in any key, any time. Give it a shot! The rewards are well worth the effort.

Here is an example of the I9, with a passing ♭9, leading to the IV chord:

This one goes back and forth between I7 and V7sus4. Believe it or not, the V7sus4 chord acts like a I chord rather than a V chord. This is because it has no 3rd , which in this case would be the note B. The rest of the notes end up sounding like extensions on the I chord (D=9, F=11 and A=13). And, not to be slighted, the 4 in the V7sus4 chord is the root of the I chord (in this case, C). The rhythmic alignment of the quarter-note triplets is shown with grey arrows.

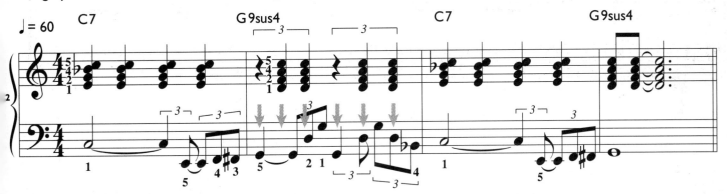

CHORDING THE MINOR CLIMB

Some blues progressions include harmonization of the bass line as it walks from one chord to the next. Here are examples of *minor climbs* used in two different places within a twelve-bar blues progression. The minor climb, or *climb-up*, is just another way to get from I to IV or V by ascending in stepwise motion with minor 7 chords.

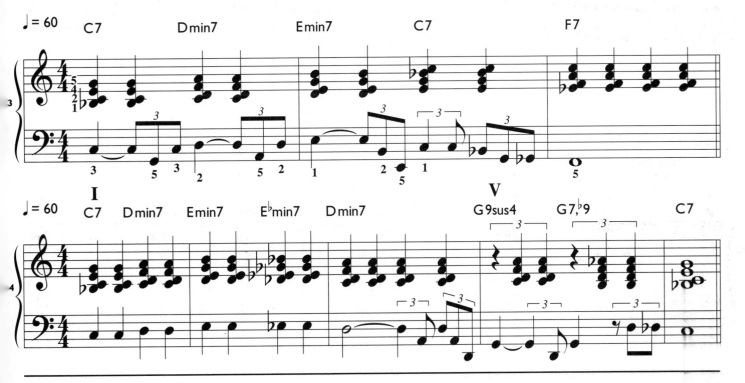

You are probably starting to sense that the simple twelve-bar progression you learned in the *Beginning* section can lead to a lot of different possibilities. It's important to become familiar with many different ways of getting through a blues progression. Some famous tunes are associated with a specific set of slow-blues changes. On the other hand, there may be several different recorded versions, each with different changes! (That's why you need to be constantly checking out recordings!) On the gig, a singer might only say "...slow blues in G..." and then count it off. The band will start playing and everyone has to collectively make choices about which chord changes to play (or follow one person's lead). If you can't lead the band clearly through the changes, or follow another player's lead, you'll be in trouble.

The chart below shows possible variations on the twelve-bar progression for a slow blues. This chart assumes a traditional blues situation. In the *Mastering* section, you'll learn some other possibilities associated with a jazz blues style.

SLOW BLUES VARIATIONS

Measure:	1	2	3	4	5	6
Possible harmonies:	I7 - V7sus4	I7 - V7sus4	I7 - ii7	iii7 - I7	IV7	$\sharp$iv°
	I7	IV7	iii - VI7	v7 - I7		$\flat$VII7

Measure:	7	8	9	10	11	12
Possible harmonies:	I7/V	iii7 - VI7	ii7-iii7-IV-$\sharp$iv°	V7sus4	I7 - vi7	ii7
	I7 - ii7	VI7	ii7	V7	I7 - VI7	II7 - V7
		iii7 - $\flat$iii7	V7	IV7	I7 - IV7	I7 - V7

Let's look at a few spots in the diagram that may look unfamiliar to you:

In bar 4, there's a minor v chord. That v7 and the I7 following it function like a ii-V leading to the IV chord—as if the IV chord were a new tonic (I).

In bar 7, the I chord might be over a 5th in the bass (in other words, in 2nd inversion). Look at the bass motion this creates in bars 4 through 8: IV, $\sharp$IV, V, VI. It sounds good! Always think of harmonic motion as being a combination of melodies, with each note of each chord belonging to a melody. It will make your harmony smoother.

Bar 9 contains a climb-up with a chord on every beat. Remember, blues might be played at such a wide range of tempos that the same basic chord progression can become a whole different animal. The slower it is, the more harmonies you can play. Some tempos may be too brisk for anything complicated.

The means of varying chord progressions seem to be endless. Earlier, we saw an example of back and forth motion with sus chords; you moved away from the I chord, then back (example 71, page 145). This is a way of adding interest and motion to a slow progression. Neighboring chords can be used in a similar manner.

Another use of neighboring chords is to lead to a new chord in the progression.

Following are chord changes to a slow blues in G, in the style of the classic tune *Stormy Monday*. On the next page, you will play an accompaniment with these changes, and a piano solo over the changes. Before going on, memorize the chord progression. Translate the progression into Roman numerals and memorize it so you can play it in any key.

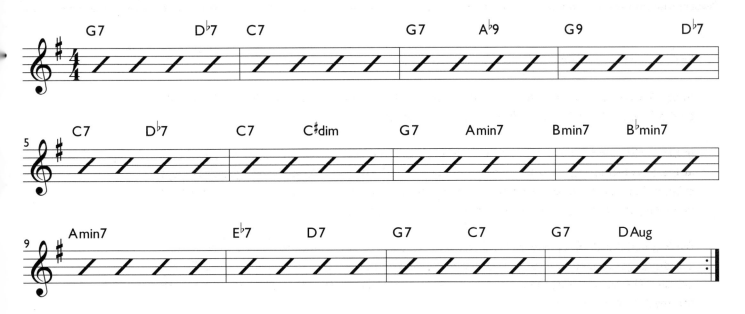

This is an example of an accompaniment for a slow blues in the style of *Stormy Monday*. If you play along with the CD, you will be playing with a rhythm section that is backing up a guitar player. In this case, you should omit the left-hand part and play only occasional roots, or nothing, in your left hand.

STORMY TUESDAY

Here is *Stormy Tuesday* again, this time written as a piano solo. With all of those chord changes, it may seem like playing a solo over a slow blues would be a nightmare. The good news is that the melodic voice doesn't need to worry about all the chord changes. Remember that the blues is about tension. The sound of the elegant and complex chord motion against familiar blues sounds (like the blues scale) is part of what makes slow blues so moving.

The left-hand part of this piece is written assuming there is a bass player. The voicings are placed above

the bass's range to stay out of its way, and many of the chord voicings don't have roots (rootless voicings are also covered in the next chapter). Look at each chord voicing and identify all of the chord tones. Remember that the goal is to learn to create your own accompaniments. You can play along with the CD, or if you wish to play this as a solo piano piece, you may use the left-hand part from the previous page or create your own part using the left-hand techniques you have learned so far.

Play the written chorus, then improvise your own solo on the changes. (Hint: you don't need to play all of the chords in your left hand).

STORMY SOLO
Track 35

CHAPTER 6

Grooving

The piano is a percussion instrument. As a piano player, you're a member of that esteemed part of the band known as the rhythm section. And any rhythm section player will tell you that the rhythm section is the most important part of the band because we make the groove happen!

You need to know how to lay down or complement the groove in the right way at the right time, and that means two things:
1. Knowing where the beat is.
2. Knowing how to accentuate the feel.

Of course, you've already done lots of grooving. You've been your own rhythm section. You've played swing eighths, straight eighths and triplet feel. The next steps are to get more comfortable playing on any part of the beat, experiment with *syncopation* (playing off the beats) and learn several comping possibilities for a number of different grooves. You'll soon be welcoming opportunities to be groovemeister at the keyboard. Furthermore, as a skilled comper, you will be in great demand!

REVIEW OF RHYTHMIC FEELS

Let's review some different grooves. The definition of each feel will include two things: 1) rhythmic fundamentals; and 2) a description of a typical bass part. Good keyboard parts are a result of complementing and accentuating these two things.

SHUFFLE

Your old friend the shuffle is marked by a strong triplet feel and a strong *backbeat*, which means the second and fourth beats of each bar are emphasized in the drum part. Shuffle bass patterns typically outline the chord, using a swing eighth rhythm.

SWING

The eighth notes in a swing feel are swung, but the triplet feel is not necessarily emphasized. The main emphasis is on the quarter note—four beats per bar. The backbeat is present (the drummer plays the high-hat on 2 and 4) but not heavily emphasized.
The bass generally walks:

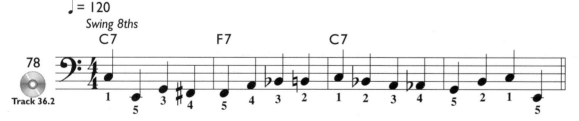

SLOW ¹²⁄₈

Combine a triplet feel with a walking bass line and decrease the tempo for a slow blues. The drummer emphasizes the quarter note and the triplet feel simultaneously.

THE TWO FEEL

A variation on swing. Instead of marking every quarter note, only 1 and 3 are emphasized (sounding like two beats per measure). Up-tempo swing tunes sometimes start out in a two feel. The bass plays simply—mainly on beats 1 and 3, alternating roots and chord tones.

SECOND-LINE GROOVE

Second line is the name given a rhythm the drummers in the second line of a New Orleans funeral procession played. The eighth-note feel is somewhere between straight and swung. The backbone of second-line groove is this dotted-quarter note pattern:

Bass parts for second-line grooves are based on the same pattern:

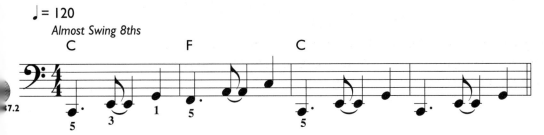

Chapter 8, on New Orleans-style piano, covers second-line rhythms in more detail.

FUNK

The basic elements of funk grooves are straight eighths, a strong feeling of four and sixteenth note creativity. Having your sixteenth note rhythms together is an important part of being a competent modern blues and R&B player.

RHUMBA

Afro-Cuban in origin, rhumba-inspired rhythms have been incorporated into both blues and jazz. The feel is similar to a second-line groove but the eighth notes are completely straight.

SWINGTIME

When you play a blues with a swing feel, and there's a bass player walking a line, your role in the groove-making is more open than when playing a shuffle. Since you don't have to play the bass line, you become a colorist, enhancing both groove and harmony and there is a great deal of flexibility in what you can play. You might choose to use jazz-influenced rhythms and chord voicings because you're playing in a jazz-like feel.

Rootless Voicings

Chord voicings used with a swing feel tend to include more extensions and alterations and frequently omit the root, allowing the bass player flexibility in composing a walking line.

Here is a commonly played rootless voicing for a G13 chord:

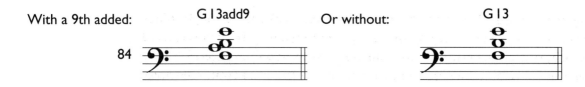

The same voicing might include alterations.

Here is a commonly played voicing for a 9th chord:

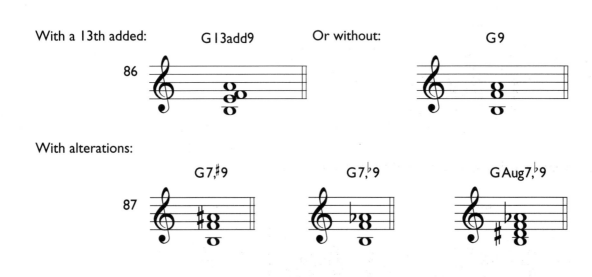

Exercises:

Learn the above voicings in all twelve keys. Play them first as three-note voicings (leaving out a 9th or 13th) and then as four-note voicings. Play them again, altering one extension at a time. Listen carefully to the sound of each voicing against the root (play the root with your other hand). You should be able to play the voicings with either your right or your left hand.

A WORD ABOUT RANGE

As you played the rootless voicings in different keys, you probably noticed that you had to move up or down an octave at some point to keep things from getting either too muddy or too high. You will naturally gravitate to playing certain voicings more frequently in certain keys, based on the range where it sounds best. There is no hard and fast rule about what is correct. It will depend upon many factors, including what keyboard sound you are playing (an electric piano or organ sound, for instance, will sound muddier below middle C than an acoustic piano), what other instruments you're playing with, etc. Trust your ears. If it doesn't sound good, find another way to play it.

RHYTHMIC RESOLUTION

In the *Beginning* section we discussed the use of tension and resolution in blues melodies and harmony. The same concepts may be applied to rhythms. Tension is created by playing off the beat; resolution occurs on the beats (see "Syncopation" on page 154). The concept of rhythmic tension and resolution is employed constantly to make a swing tune *swing*. Below are some examples of how it is used:

Anticipation of the next chord.

Use of a neighboring chord (harmonic anticipation) in combination with rhythmic anticipation.

Combining off-beats and on-beats to accentuate the swing feel.

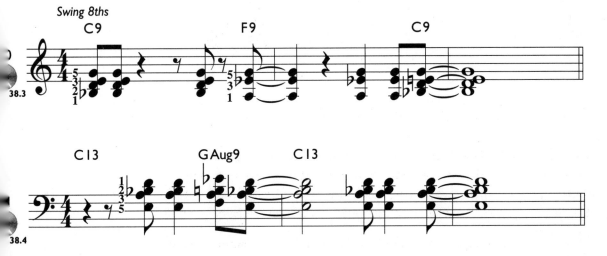

SYNCOPATION

Another name for rhythmic tension is *syncopation*. Syncopation is what happens when the accent or emphasis is shifted to a weak beat or weak part of a beat. For example, if we begin a tone on an off-beat (the "and" of a beat) and continue it through the on-beat with a tie or dot, the effect is one of syncopation.

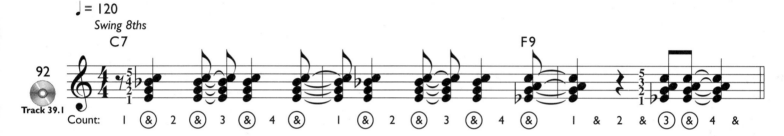

Syncopated rhythms may begin on any of these different subdivisions that is not on a beat.

You can use syncopation to increase the rhythmic tension by starting on an off-beat and playing a string of notes (or chords) with equal rhythmic value, thus crossing on-beats and bar lines until resolution is desired.

EIGHTH NOTES

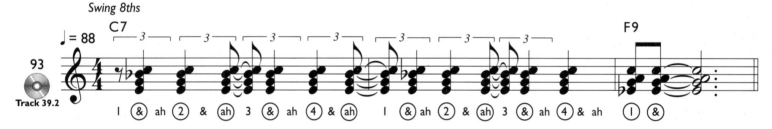

EIGHTH NOTE TRIPLETS

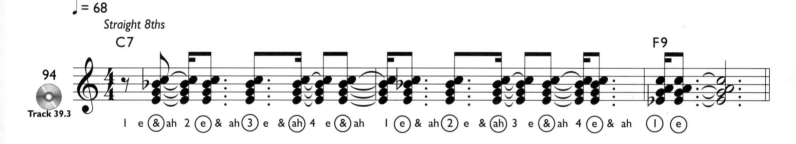

SIXTEENTH NOTES

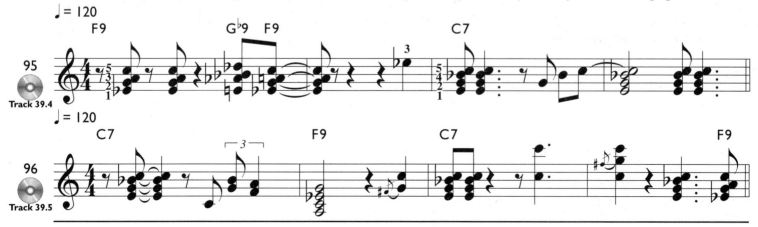

PUTTING IT ALL TOGETHER

Remember that you have a large selection of blues sounds to choose from when comping. You can play more than just chords. A well-placed single note, octave or melodic fragment might be the perfect spice for a swinging blues.

Sister Swing is a swing blues with a two-handed piano accompaniment. A guitar part is provided and a bass player can fit right in. Play along with the CD, or call up your blues-playing friends and try out your new voicings on them.

Exercises:

After playing the written accompaniment to *Sister Swing*, make up your own comping ideas and play them along with the rhythm tracks on the CD.

It's time to get into sixteenth notes and get funky. Lots of modern blues artists, such as B.B. King and Buddy Guy, play twelve-bar blues tunes with funky straight-eighth grooves. Think sixteenth notes instead of triplet feel.

The bass player might play the following:

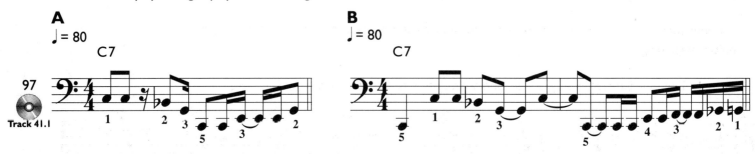

There are many ways to comp for the type of groove shown in example 97B. You can reinforce the downbeat (1), or you can leave it alone and play off any other part of any beat in the bar.

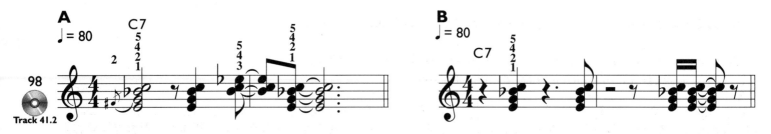

If both you and a guitar are comping, don't play the same thing as the guitar. For example, if the guitar plays a figure starting on the first beat, accent the end of the bar (or vice versa).

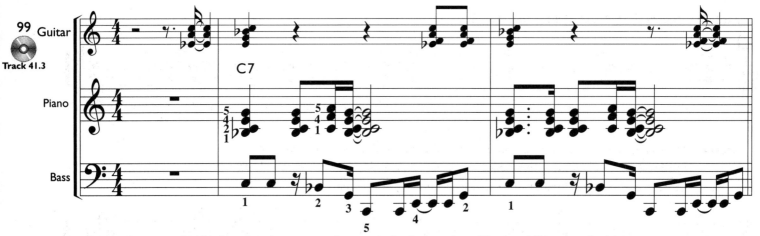

Repetition is probably the most important element in funk comping. Choose a figure and stick with it. The simplest idea can add a lot if it is always played in the same place in the groove.

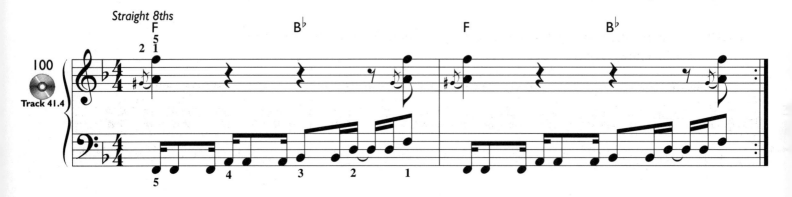

RHYTHMIC EXERCISES

To get your inner metronome working, and get the rhythmic sixteenth-note ideas flowing, systematically practice playing on different parts of the beat. To begin with, count sixteenth notes as "one-ee-and-ah." As you get more comfortable with subdivisions, you'll begin to feel each part of the beat without counting.

Set your metronome to 60 and make sure you can play steady sixteenth notes at that tempo before beginning.

Step 1: For four bars, play only the second sixteenth note of each beat.

Steps 2 and 3: Do the same thing with the third and fourth parts of the beat.

Step 4: Play on the on-beats for one bar, on the second part of each beat for the next bar, on the third part for the next bar, etc.

Step 5: Repeat Step 4, but change on every beat.

Step 6: Now create a rhythm with a combination of parts of the beat. You can do it randomly if you like. For example, try playing on the downbeat, the fourth part of beat 2, the second part of beat 3 and the third part of beat 4.

Step 7: Try syncopation—a repetition of dotted eighth notes, for example (play every third sixteenth note).

Al Kooper's first big break came in the 1960s, when he played on Bob Dylan's Like a Rolling Stone. *Later, he performed with Michael Bloomfield on the landmark blues album, "Super Session."*

Here's a funky blues tune that will challenge your counting skills. It's a comp for the guitar part provided. Play along with the CD or get a friend to jam with.

IN A BLUE FUNK

Track 43

THE IN-BETWEEN ZONE

There are shuffles, swing tunes, slow blues and funk tunes, and then there are tunes that don't
fit strictly into any of those categories. Some blues grooves incorporate aspects of second-line
rhythms (page 151) and other unusual grooves, but might retain an element of a swing or shuffle
feel as well. You can generally comp to these sorts of grooves using an adaptation of what you
already know. As long as you are aware of what's going on (in other words—listen carefully
to what the bass and drums are playing), you can use your ears, your existing vocabulary and
a bit of creativity to play something cool.

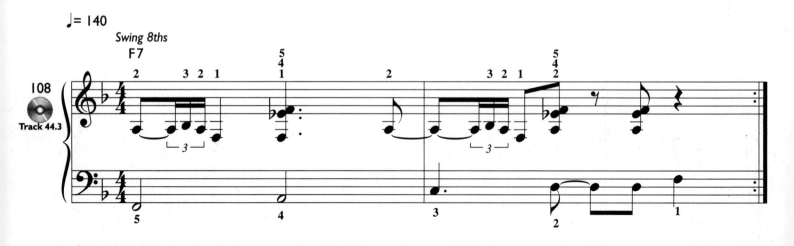

He's Into Something is in the style of the rhumba-like Muddy Waters composition, *She's Into Something.*

Track 45

HE'S INTO SOMETHING

♩= 100

Almost Straight 8ths

CHAPTER 7

Chicago Breakdown

The Chicago era played such a huge role in the evolution of blues that when people speak of playing the blues, they are often thinking of the Chicago sound. Much of the material you've been working on is derived from Chicago style blues. The shuffle, the triplet figures, blues scale licks, playing with a guitar and bass, playing fills—these are all elements of Chicago blues. This chapter will take you more deeply into that style.

Several decades ago in Chicago, an extraordinary combination of circumstances combined to create an even more extraordinary musical phenomenon. These circumstances resulted in the evolution of urban blues as we know it, which in turn had a large hand in shaping the course of American pop music.

THE CHICAGO BLUES STORY

MIGRATION

In the decade following World War I there was a trend away from agriculture and towards industry. The result was a tremendous migration from the South to the North, specifically to the North's industrial centers. The largest migration was from Alabama, Mississippi, Tennessee, Kentucky, Arkansas and Louisiana. The vast majority of those relocating were Black Americans. They travelled via the railroad and their primary destinations were Chicago, Detroit and Ohio. The Illinois Central was by far the most travelled route. It ran from New Orleans to Chicago. This train took in the whole of Delta blues country.

RENT PARTIES

Hundreds of musicians who had already forsaken their sharecropper existences and taken to the road as performers—playing in barrelhouses and honkytonks throughout the South—were among those who moved to Chicago in search of work. The immigrant flow was forcing rents up, which led to *rent parties*. These were parties where admission was charged and used to cover rent. Piano and guitar duos were popular at these parties and this is how the early blues pianists in Chicago worked.

EARLY PLAYERS ON THE SCENE

The early Chicago blues scene was dominated by two guitarist/vocalists: Big Bill Broonzy and Tampa Red. The major piano players of those times all seem to have worked with Big Bill or Tampa Red at some point. They were "Cripple" Clarence Lofton, Blind John Davis, Tommy A. Dorsey and, most notably, Big Maceo Merriweather and Roosevelt Sykes—two huge influences on developing pianists in Chicago. They played rent parties and recorded for labels like Melotone, Vocalion and Okeh. Boogie pianists Albert Ammons and Meade Lux Lewis were roommates in Chicago in the 1930s, playing rent parties and driving taxis. Jimmy Yancey lived in Chicago but was rarely in the spotlight there.

BETWEEN WARS

Prohibition and a strong organized crime element in Chicago led to a thriving club scene. For Black musicians in America, underground operations offered the best opportunities for work because common discriminatory practices did not apply. In the late 1930s, jazz became popular and began to influence Chicago blues. The extraordinary amount of blues piano talent in Chicago, however, along with the addition of harmonica players to the sound, actually pulled Chicago blues away from the influence of jazz, allowing it to develop independently.

INDEPENDENT LABELS

Small, independent record companies sprang up and thrived in Chicago. Recordings of Black artists at that time were called *race records*. They were not played by white DJs and not promoted to white audiences. But the independent labels saw and developed a market for race records that grew quickly. This market was able to support a number of small labels through the 1930s, '40s and '50s.

POST-WAR CHICAGO BLUES

The sound in Chicago after World War II was urban and electric. Vocal artists like Muddy Waters, Howlin' Wolf and Elmore James dominated the town with their bands. These artists recorded for Chess records, which had the best artists and the most hits. The strongest piano players played for these artists. Otis Spann and Johnnie Jones—both influenced by Big Maceo—were the most well-known. Otis Span was Muddy Waters' pianist for a long time. Johnny Jones played with Muddy Waters, Howlin' Wolf and Elmore James. Sunnyland Slim, while not frequently recorded, was a strong presence on the scene and reportedly arranged the session that introduced Muddy Waters to the Chess brothers. Ike Turner discovered Howlin' Wolf and played with him on *Moanin' at Midnight*. This hit record resulted in a battle between record labels which was eventually won by Chess and led to the Wolf's arrival in Chicago as Muddy Waters' biggest competition. Little Brother Montgomery, Roosevelt Sykes' life-long friend, arrived in Chicago not too long after his buddy Roosevelt. Little Brother recorded with Otis Rush (Cobra and Chess records). Lafayette Leake also played with Otis Rush and Howlin' Wolf. Memphis Slim modelled himself after his hero, Roosevelt Sykes, and followed him to Chicago, playing with Big Bill Broonzy in the 1940s before developing his own band.

THE 1960s AND BEYOND

In the '60s, success for the small labels became more difficult as interest in the blues waned. The late 1960s saw a revival in interest, but it was a white audience discovering blues through the efforts of historians. This interest allowed established players, like Muddy Waters and Memphis Slim, to enjoy lengthy touring careers, but the electricity of the club and recording scene of the earlier Chicago era would not be repeated. Players in later years included Pinetop Perkins and Big Moose Walker, both of whom performed with Muddy Waters. Big Moose Walker played the organ, an instrument which became extremely popular with blues guitarists, perhaps exceeding the piano as the blues keyboard of choice.

The blues on Chicago's south side reflected a hard-working and restless urban population. The music was loud, aggressive and driving. Blues pianists were incredibly rhythmic, even though their left hand responsibilities had diminished as bass players began to fill that role. Piano players moved their rhythmic ideas into the right hand, playing the mid-upper and upper ranges of the piano, where they would "cut" through a loud band with a heavy mid-range. The sounds were barked out in a way that made the piano just as effective at speaking the urgency of the blues as any other instrument in the band.

Let's look at how we can thicken some of the figures and licks you've already learned for some real Chicago sounds.

Recall working on harmonic development (see Chapter 2). Combine your favorite sound with some variation in rhythmic density (play triplets) to make an interesting musical phrase.

Rather than only playing a 4th or a 5th in his right hand, Otis Spann sometimes played triplets with a 7th or 9th interval. A 5th might be included inside the larger interval.

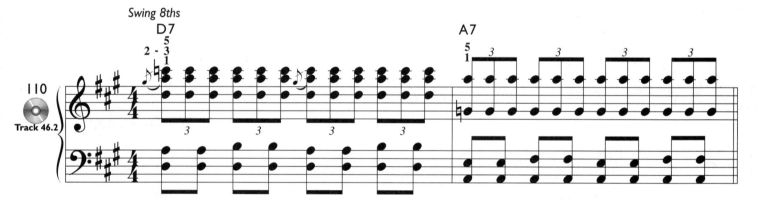

Or he would make a melodic/rhythmic figure out of a "bent note" within an octave.

Nest a classic melodic lick within a dyad (two-note chord) like this sound in the style of Maceo Merriweather's masterpiece, *Chicago Breakdown*:

"Fall off" with a descending glissando (another Otis Spann technique). Lead your gliss down the piano by closing your hand, bringing your thumb and first finger together.

String your licks together to make runs down the piano.

These exercises will help you prepare to play the lick in example 114:

Put interesting harmonic devices (like parallel 6ths) into a Chicago-style rhythmic context. This example is in the style of Lafayette Leake:

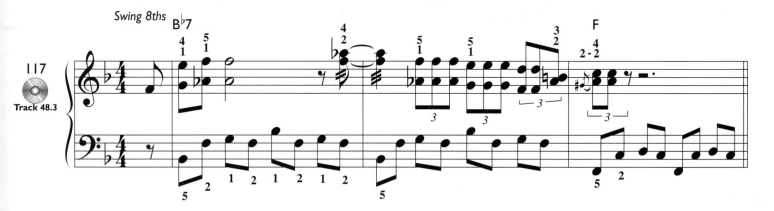

VARIATIONS ON A CLASSIC SOUND

On page 116, you learned a classic V-I resolving lick in twelve keys. The following examples demonstrate the unique twists different Chicago pianists gave this lick:

In the style of Maceo Merriweather

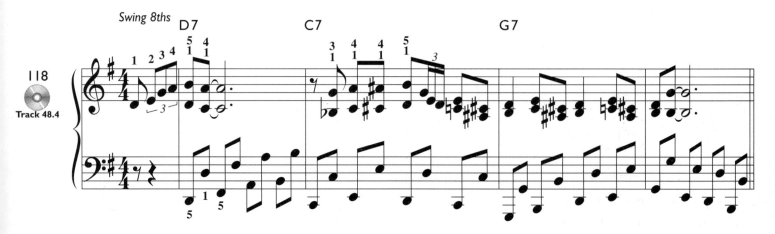

In the style of Lafayette Leake

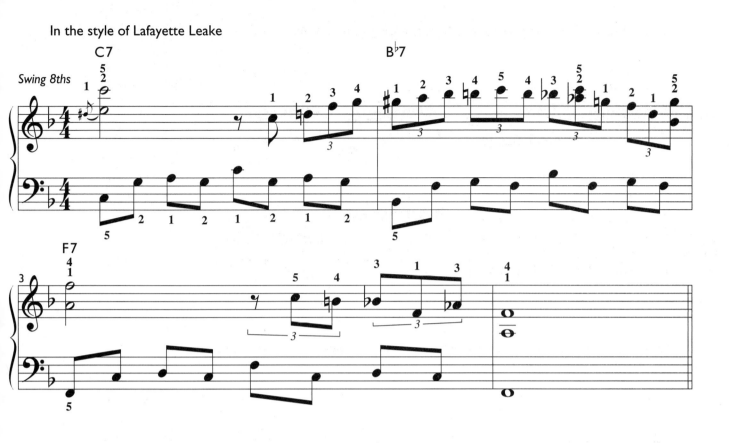

In the style of Otis Spann

BREAKS

There was a great deal of variety in the form and arrangement of tunes being performed and recorded during Chicago's thriving blues era. Muddy Waters' band, especially, set a precedent with sophisticated grooves, interesting introductions and endings and varied forms. Many of the songs included *breaks* of various lengths and at different points in the form. A break—a place in the music where the band stops and the soloist fills—was sometimes preceded by a specific riff unique to that song.

BREAKS IN AN OPENING LINE

BREAK ON IV CHORD (BAR 10 OF A TWELVE-BAR BLUES)

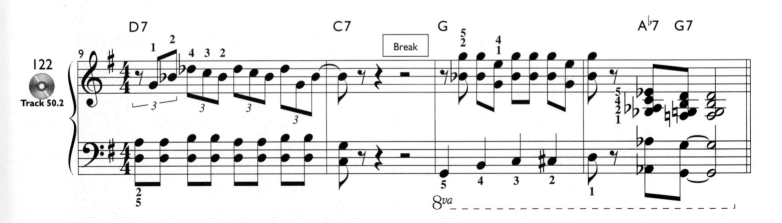

BREAK IN BAR 7 OF A SIXTEEN-BAR BLUES

The twelve-bar blues and eight-bar blues were not the only blues forms. Others included songs that stayed on the I chord the whole time (John Lee Hooker, Howlin' Wolf and Muddy Waters all played songs like this) and songs that were sixteen bars long, revolving around the I for eight bars, and then following the last eight bars of a twelve bar blues. These sixteen-bar forms frequently included a break in bar 7:

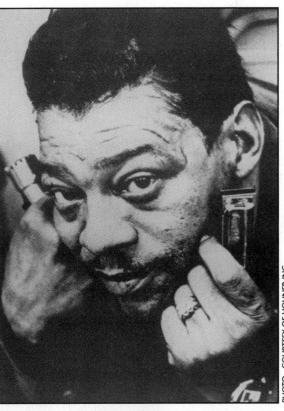

Little Walter *is thought by many to be the most influential harmonica player ever. He left his mark on the Chicago scene playing with Muddy Waters (starting in 1948). His playing displayed almost a jazz sound over swinging blues backgrounds. His phrasing is reminiscent of a jazz saxophonist and his amplified sound revolutionized blues harmonica.*

I Feel So Chicago is a sixteen-bar blues in the style of a Bill Broonzy tune recorded by Muddy Waters called *I Feel So Good*. Otis Rush recorded a similar tune with a funk feel written by Chuck Willis called *I Feel So Bad*. The guitar solo (pages 170 and 171) is followed by a piano solo (pages 172 and 173).

I FEEL SO CHICAGO

The bass player in your band would probably play this:

Swing 8ths

CHAPTER 8

New Orleans

THE NEW ORLEANS BLUES STORY

By the turn of the century, "the Crescent City" (New Orleans) was alive with a wide range of new sounds, reflecting the changing times and the city's diverse culture. Blues and ragtime shook barrelhouses; parade music blossomed into jazz that was soon floating from Mississippi river boats; singers like Mahalia Jackson merged spiritual, jazz and blues inflections together; and Jelly Roll Morton experimented with improvisation.

The New Orleans piano style reflects these varied origins. While blues-based, there is a preference for eight-bar forms (and multiples of eight bars) rather than twelve-bar forms. Like jazz, the harmony is European flavored with strong church influences. The rhythms, however, are syncopated and primarily African in origin. Over several decades, players melded these influences into a cohesive New Orleans sound. While a new urban blues sound was evolving in Chicago, in New Orleans artists like Professor Longhair, Fats Domino, Allan Tousaint, Huey "Piano" Smith and Dr. John were laying down danceable grooves on the piano that would form the roots of rhythm and blues (R&B) and rock'n'roll.

On page 151, you learned to recognize a second-line rhythm. This is the rhythm most frequently associated with the New Orleans sound.

New Orleans Rock is in the style of *Iko Iko,* a Dr. John song written by James Sugarboy Crawford.

NEW ORLEANS ROCK

Track 53

♩ = 138

Straight 8ths

Fine

D.S. al Fine

You probably recognized many of the sounds in *New Orleans Rock*. The form is different from a typical blues but still built from dominant chords. The melodies are based on the major pentatonic scale and once again, we are playing the familiar resolving V-I lick. You'll get lots of mileage from variations on and extensions of this sound. Check out these examples:

OCTAVES AND ORNAMENTATION

Like other blues piano styles, New Orleans piano uses devices to create a big, full sound. These include lots of octave doublings, ornamentations and trilled chords.

Professor Longhair broke up the sound by inserting dramatic climbups (or down) to the IV chord. These climbups often have a different rhythmic feel than the principal groove of the tune.

Climbup to the IV Chord in C

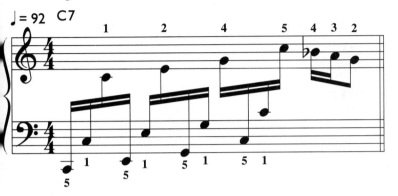

Another Climbup to the IV Chord in C

The Two Hands Moving in Opposite Directions to the IV Chord (counterpoint)

Tipitina is a well-known eight-bar, New Orleans-style blues. *Longhair Blues* is in the style of *Tipitina*.

THE LEFT HAND

The bass line to *Longhair Blues* combines a boogie-woogie line with a syncopated dotted-eighth note pattern. The first part is in the style of a Jimmy Yancey line, but with straight eighths. There are also some dotted-eighth note figures. Count the rhythm by subdividing to sixteenth notes:

3-e-&-ah 4-e-&-ah

The left-hand part also includes walking lines with broken octaves. Before playing the piece, work on just the left hand with a metronome until you are comfortable with it.

 LONGHAIR BLUES

Track 56

A big part of what makes New Orleans music sound so cool is the rhythm. *New Orleans Rock* and *Longhair Blues* gave you a feeling for playing syncopated left-hand rhythms against different right-hand figures. Players like Professor Longhair and Dr. John had highly developed independence between the hands and incredible rhythmic variation in their playing.

MORE ON THE LEFT HAND

The left hand in New Orleans style piano does several things at once: it lays down the groove; it outlines the harmony; and it accentuates the melody with fills and internal harmonic voices. One of the great challenges of playing in the New Orleans style is to carefully arrange a tune and then be able to play the rhythm correctly—with ease, so that it grooves.

Think of the left hand as a combination of a repeated groove and improvised lines (as you composed walking lines, for instance). Using your ear as a guide, let the left-hand part be a melting pot for sounds you've acquired: walking, playing 10ths, 7ths, octaves, adding fills, etc. Let techniques you've applied in the right hand show up in the left. The grace note, for example:

Or holding a note while playing a figure with other fingers:

Here is a sample left-hand part for an eight-bar blues. Notice that the bass line in the first of each two-bar pair generally provides the groove, while the second provides a transition to a new chord.

Exercises:

Write your own New Orleans-style eight-bar blues. Choose a groove-pattern first, then let your ears guide you in breaking up the pattern with fills.

Many of the bass lines in New Orleans piano music came from boogie-woogie. Some of the earliest boogie-woogie sounds were the roots of contemporary R&B. For example, this bass pattern in the style of *Pinetop's Boogie*—a very early boogie tune by Pine Top Smith—was recycled by Dr. John into his funky 1970s hit, *Qualified*.

In the next example, the right-hand figure that parallels the bass line adds to the groove by including motion within each chord. This type of figure is basic vocabulary for R&B grooves.

Here is the same motion but descending as a comping groove on the IV chord:

The key to this type of comping is to know the key well and keep the notes diatonic. Here is a similar figure as used on a minor tune:

Crescent City Groove is in the style of Pinetop's *Boogie* and *Qualified.*

CRESCENT CITY GROOVE

Track 59

CHAPTER 9

West Coast "Lounge Blues" and the Birth of Soul

BACKGROUND

Postwar California sprouted its own blues/jazz scene fertilized by a number of Texas transplants, among them the highly influential guitarist T-Bone Walker and singer/pianists Charles Brown, Amos Milburn and Floyd Dixon. Another popular singer and pianist was Los Angeles native Hadda Brooks, whose first recording, "Swinging the Boogie," was the motivation for Jules Bihari's founding of Modern Records. At the center of the scene was an Oklahoman guitarist named Lowell Fulsom, best known for his recording of *Everyday I Have the Blues*. Both Charles Brown and pianist Lloyd Glenn played with Fulsom, and subbing for Glenn on occasion (sometimes being mistaken for him) was the versatile young Ray Charles.

Artists like Charles Brown and Ray Charles played in a cool, laid-back manner. They were indebted to Nat King Cole for their vocal styles. They combined traditional Southern blues with sophisticated jazz sounds and gospel influences. This new style was a departure from the old boogie-woogie and barrelhouse piano traditions, where the left hand drove the rhythm incessantly. Many of the West Coast "club blues" or "lounge blues" tunes were played with a swing feel. The players added subtle left-hand, jazz piano style accompaniments, complementing their right-hand ideas with rootless voicings. They were still steeped in the blues, however—minor and major pentatonic scales and classic blues licks were the main ingredients in the improvised lines, but with a mellower mood.

"LOUNGE BLUES" SOUNDS

After earning a chemistry degree in Texas, Charles Brown moved to California and focused on his music career. He developed a style that would influence many young pianists, including Ray Charles and Amos Milburn (who gave Aladdin Records eleven R&B hits between 1949 and 1953). Working early-on with The Three Blazers (with guitarist Johnny Moore and bass player Eddie Williams), Brown eventually launched a successful solo career that produced hits like *Driftin' Blues, Merry Christmas Baby* and *Black Nights*.

Here are a few trademark Charles Brown sounds:

1. ROLLED CHORDS
Larger chords can be tremoloed or "rolled" in a similar manner to the two-note figures you played in Chicago-style blues. Charles Brown sometimes sustained a roll through several chord changes.

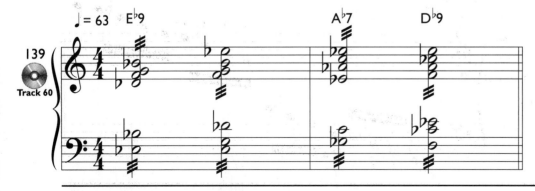

2. HARMONIC/MELODIC MOTION WITH 10THS

3. GOSPEL-TYPE COMPING, ESPECIALLY IN A ¹²⁄₈ FEEL

4. PENTATONIC LICKS

These were played in a more fluid, less rhythmically-driving style than the Chicago pianists played. Like B.B. King, Brown favors the major pentatonic scale, except on minor blues. Here's a turnaround in C:

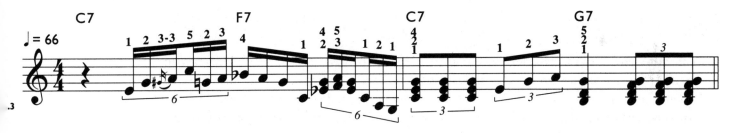

5. REPEATED CHORDS IN DIFFERENT OCTAVES

6. CLASSICAL-TYPE ARPEGGIOS

This is another church-derived sound.

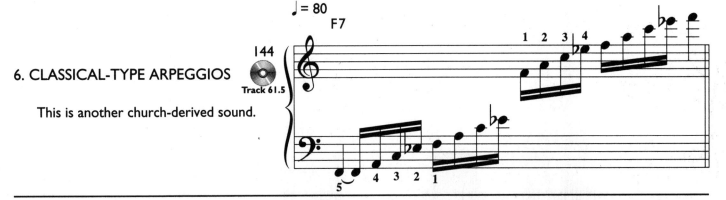

Ray Charles incorporated much of Charles Brown's style, but Charles' playing was more diverse, including heavy gospel influences at times and shades of jazz at others.

Example 145 is a gospel figure in the style of Ray Charles. He played this type of line often in $\frac{12}{8}$ tunes.

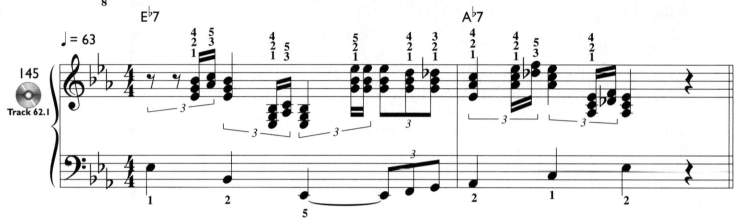

He played elegant lines over jazz standards.

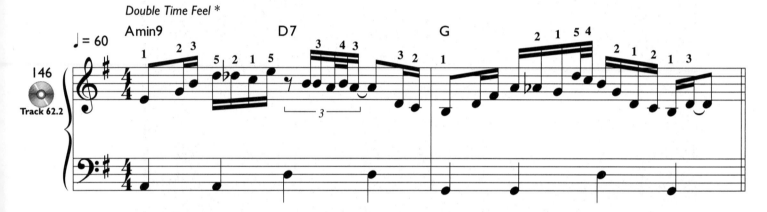

* "Double-time feel" means the sixteenth notes feel like eighth notes. In this case, they are swung.

Lines like this one, played over a swing groove, combined it all into a cohesive, sophisticated sound:

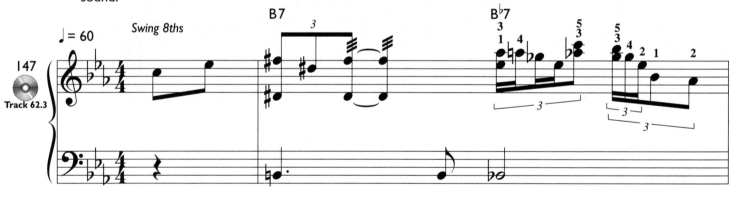

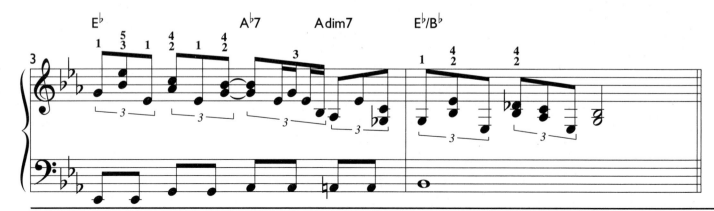

*Sometimes called the "father of soul," **Ray Charles** blended gospel music and blues from the deep South with West Coast jazz-blues to create his own sound. Afflicted by glaucoma at age 5, Charles was blind by age 7. At age 17, Charles moved to Seattle and came under the influence of the developing West Coast "lounge blues" sound. A young Ray Charles styled his vocals after Nat King Cole and Charles Brown, but in later years developed his own, slightly edgier style. His first recordings were for Swingtime Records. His first R&B hit, in 1949, was* Confession Blues. *Charles signed with Atlantic in 1952. He recorded hits in several categories of music and grew in popularity with several age groups over the next few decades. Never a purist, Ray Charles espoused versatility. Happily wedding his musical influences, he performed Tin-Pan Alley tunes, blues or jazz standards as he saw fit.*

Heartbreak Blues is in the style of a Charles Brown tune, *I Want to Go Home*, as Charles Brown or Ray Charles might have played it. Notice the $\frac{12}{8}$ time signature. Feel it in four big beats, with the dotted-quarter note equaling one beat.

HEARTBREAK BLUES

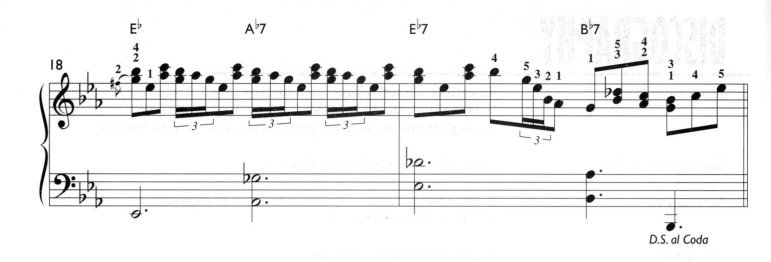

D.S. al Coda

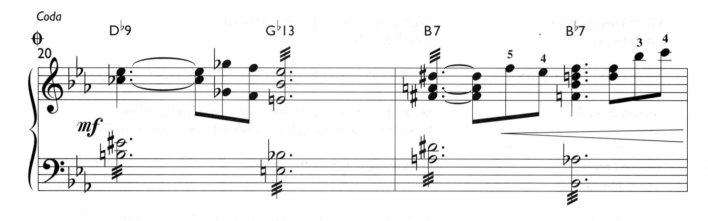

DISCOGRAPHY

Atlantic Blues Four-CD set including blues piano compilation with Jimmy Yancey, Professor Longhair, Meade Lux Lewis, etc. There is also great piano playing on the vocal and guitar compilations. (Atlantic Records)

Blues by Roosevelt Sykes Roosevelt Sykes. (Smithsonian Folkways)

Blues Essentials Compilation with Muddy Waters, Elmore James, Memphis Slim, Howlin Wolf, etc. (Capitol Records)

Birth of Soul Ray Charles. (Atlantic Records)

Boogie Woogie, Stride and Piano Blues With Pete Johnson, James P. Johnson, etc. (EMI Records)

Dr. John Plays Mac Rebenack Dr. John. (Rounder Records) Solo piano. (Clean Cuts Records)

Essential Blues Piano Great blues piano compilation with Otis Spann, Lafayette Leake, Pinetop Perkins, Katie Webster, etc. (House of Blues)

Hoochie Coochie Man/ Got My Mojo Workin' Jimmy Smith. (Verve Records)

Jump Back Honey Hadda Brooks. The complete Okeh sessions (Columbia)

Live and Well Live at the Regal B.B. King. (MCA Records)

New Orleans Piano Professor Longhair. (Atlantic)

Memphis Slim Memphis Slim. (Chess MCA Records)

Patriarch of the Blues Sunnyland Slim. (Opal Records)

Rekooperation Al Kooper. (BMG Music)

Spiders on the Keys James Booker (Rounder)

Texas Flood Stevie Ray Vaughan. (Epic records). Classic example of modern blues guitar.

The Blues Never Die Otis Spann. (Prestige Records)

The Chess 50th Anniversary Collection Muddy Waters. (Chess/MCA Records)

The Complete Recordings Robert Johnson. No keyboards here, but he may be the most important blues artist ever. (Columbia Records).

Vocal Accompaniment and Early Post-war Recordings: 1930-1954 Little Brother Montgomery. (Document Records)

Legend Charles Brown. (MCA Records)

Live Ray Charles. (Rhino Records)

MASTERING BLUES KEYBOARD

MERRILL CLARK

This book was acquired, edited, and produced
by Workshop Arts, Inc., the publishing arm of
the National Keyboard Workshop.
Nathaniel Gunod, editor
Joe Bouchard, music typesetter
Cathy Bolduc, interior design
Audio tracks recorded at Bar None Studio, Cheshire, CT

CONTENTS

ABOUT THE AUTHOR

Merrill Clark attended the University of Utah as a jazz theory major on full scholarship, where he studied with Dr. William Fowler and film composer Pat Williams. He graduated *Magna cum Laude* in 1978. His compositions have been performed throughout the country. He has been awarded many honors including being named "Outstanding Composer" at the 1972 American College Jazz Festival. He has been composing, performing and teaching in New York City since 1979. From 1983 to 1988, he was Director of Jazz Studies at SOJ Studios where he taught workshops, composed, arranged and recorded on keyboards, bass and guitar. In 1985, he was awarded a grant from "Meet the Composer" to present a concert of original compositions featuring jazz violinist, John Blake, Jr. Recent major compositions include a one-act opera, *Sanctuary for Two Violins Under Assault* (commissioned by Joseph Papp), a quadruple fugue for chamber orchestra entitled *Melee*, a ballet for electric viola d'amore and percussion, *The Tragedy of Tarpeia*, and a two-act opera based on Oscar Wilde's *The Picture of Dorian Gray*. Merrill is currently a solfegist on the staff at A.S.C.A.P. (The American Society of Composers, Authors and Publishers).

00

Track 1

An MP3 CD is included with this book to make learning easier and more enjoyable. The symbol shown at bottom left appears next to every example in the book that features an MP3 track. Use the MP3s to ensure you're capturing the feel of the examples and interpreting the rhythms correctly. The track number below the symbol corresponds directly to the example you want to hear (example numbers are above the icon). All the track numbers are unique to each "book" within this volume, meaning every book has its own Track 1, Track 2, and so on. (For example, *Beginning Blues Keyboard* starts with Track 1, as does *Intermediate Blues Keyboard* and *Mastering Blues Keyboard*.) Track 1 will help you tune an electronic keyboard to this CD.

The disc is playable on any CD player equipped to play MP3 CDs. To access the MP3s on your computer, place the CD in your CD-ROM drive. In Windows, double-click on My Computer, then right-click on the CD icon labeled "MP3 Files" and select Explore to view the files and copy them to your hard drive. For Mac, double-click on the CD icon on your desktop labeled "MP3 Files" to view the files and copy them to your hard drive.

INTRODUCTION

Welcome to *Mastering Blues Keyboard*, the third part of the *Complete Blues Keyboard Method*. If you have completed the *Beginning* and *Intermediate* sections of this book, you should have a solo repertoire representing many styles to perform and improvise on.

To get the most out of the *Mastering* section, you should also:

• Be able to function in a variety of ensemble formats from duos with guitarists, bassists or vocalists to being part of a complete rhythm section.

• Have at your fingertips a sizeable basic blues vocabulary of classic phrases, chord progressions, turnarounds and bass lines, as well as styles and feels.

• Be familiar with the general outline of the historical development of the blues.

• Know about some of the major figures from each period and geographical area. Hopefully, you have begun to collect recordings by the artists mentioned thus far and are spending quality time listening to them.

In this section, there will be more information of a theoretical nature. It's up to you to take each idea and find a personal way to use it. Most of the examples in this section are written in the key of C for convenience, but they should be played in all keys. For the more difficult pieces and passages, it is a good idea to learn the hands separately before combining them. Practice with a metronome. Start the study of each piece or figure slowly enough so that you can play it without mistakes. Increase the tempo gradually and, when a piece is fast enough, use the click as a back beat (on two and four of the bar only). When you play a note precisely on the click, the click will not be heard.

Playing the blues well is a lifetime pursuit. The three books of this method are just a starting point. Remain open to new possibilities and information while always maintaining your connection with the roots of the blues—the core body of skills and historical continuity that make the blues what it is. Above all, I hope that you will find this material useful, and that you will enjoy your studies.

ACKNOWLEDGEMENTS

Thanks to everyone at the National Keyboard Workshop, Nat Gunod and Joe Bouchard in particular. Thanks also to: Alan Weight; Bob Gibson; Dan Waldis; Dr. William Fowler; Ladd McIntosh; John Blake, Jr.; John Castellano; Pat Williams; Ramiro Cortes; Dr. Joyce Newman; Neal Haiduck; Steve Lynch; Richard Fairfax; Tricia Woods; Samir Chatterjee; Louis Bauzo; Steve Turre and Akua Dixon-Turre; Joe Covey; Brenda Vincent; Taleatia Shannon Vincent-Clark; all my students over the years (who completed my education); every musician I ever listened to or transcribed (I never heard anyone from whom I didn't learn something); and special thanks to Albert Bouchard, Deborah Frost and Ace.

CHAPTER 1

Review

TRIADS

A chord is a structure built from three or more notes. The most basic type of chord is a triad, a three note chord. A triad is built with a root (1), 3rd (3) and 5th (5). We learned four types of triads.

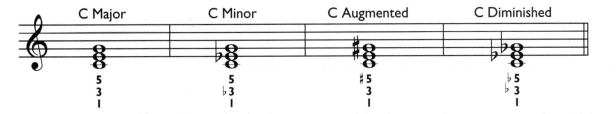

Any triad can be inverted.

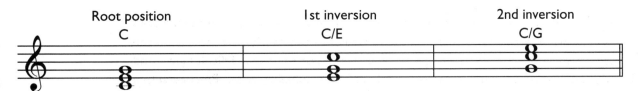

DOMINANT 7TH CHORDS

Let's look at the notes of the major scale and notice every other note:

C	D	**E**	F	**G**	A	**B**
1	2	3	4	5	6	7

We can use every other note of the scale to build a four-note chord:

C	E	G	B	
1	3	5	7	This is a **C Major 7** chord.

To make a C Dominant 7th chord, or **C7**, we lower the 7th by a half step (♭7), from B to B♭.

C	E	G	B♭	
1	3	5	♭7	This is a **C7** chord.

You also need to be able to easily invert dominant 7th chords.

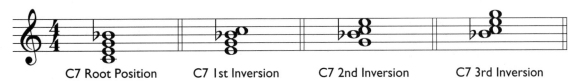

C7 Root Position   C7 1st Inversion   C7 2nd Inversion   C7 3rd Inversion

Something to notice: with the exception of root position, you always have a whole step between the dominant 7th and the root in your voicing.

So far, we have been looking at chords with four or less different notes. We can add more notes to our chords. The extra notes are called *extensions*. Extensions on a chord do not change the chord's function, but they do change its color.

Remember, we build chords in 3rds (using every other note of a scale). Following the 7th, the next chord tone is the 9th. The chart below shows the chord tones and the extensions beyond the 7th. For convenience, we'll relate it to a C root.

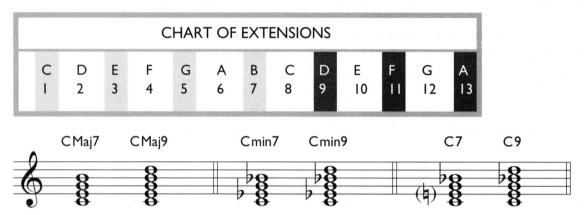

Notice that the extensions are simply the notes of the scale in the next octave. For example, the 9th is the 2nd in the next octave. Extensions give us more possibilities for voice leading because we have more notes from which to choose. We must use extensions with care, however, or they will detract from, rather than add something to, the music. Blues keyboardists frequently use 9ths as the top voice of their chords. We'll look at an example of this shortly.

Continuing up the scale past the 9th, we reach the 11th and the 13th. These are common extensions but they are not all used on all types of chords. The 11th, for instance, doesn't sound good on a major or dominant 7th chord because it clashes with the major 3rd (it is, after all, just the 4th up one octave). It sounds fine, however, on a minor chord. The 13th is used most frequently on dominant 7th chords.

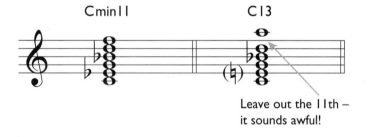

Leave out the 11th – it sounds awful!

On dominant chords, extensions may be altered by raising or lowering them a half step. The way we notate a chord with an altered extension in this book is to list the altered extension separately from the rest of the chord, placing a comma before it. Extensions are always listed from the lowest to the highest.

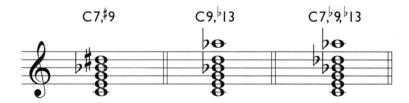

OPEN VOICINGS AND DOUBLINGS

Below is an eight-bar blues arranged with open voicings. With the exception of the first, fourth and fifth measures, each measure is voiced with a dominant 7th chord. Since dominant 7th chords have four notes (R, 3rd, 5th, ♭7th), we might expect to play two of those notes in one hand and the remaining two in the other. Generally, this is how open voicings work. There are, however, always exceptions.

Some chords have more notes than can be played at once, so we must choose what notes to leave out. With smaller chords, like triads, we may want to add notes, and so must choose what to double. Including the 5th in a chord voicing doesn't necessarily add to the sound, so we sometimes leave it out. In the first chord of bar 7 of this example, the 5th is omitted and the root is doubled. The 3rd and 7th are generally not doubled (unless one of them is the melody note). Doubling 3rds and 7ths makes things sound too muddy!

Notice that the first chord, C, is voiced as a triad rather than a dominant 7th. This is characteristic of an eight bar blues; the sound of the dominant chord is emphasized in bar 2, setting up the move to the IV chord in bar 3. The I to IV can sound like V to I.

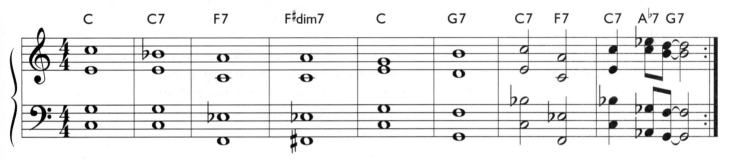

SHELL VOICINGS

Since the perfect 5th is present in Maj7, 7 and min7 chords, we don't need it to define the sound of the chord. Therefore, we can play these economical voicings with the roots in the left hand and the 3rd and 7th in the right hand. When the roots move down in 5ths (or up in 4ths), the voice leading in the right hand is very smooth.

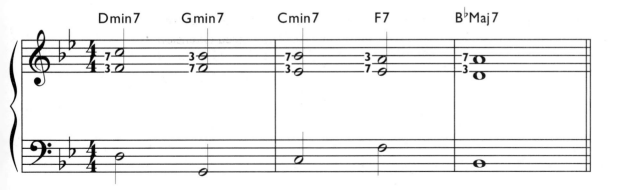

ROOTS, 3RDS, 7THS AND 10THS

In most cases, the root, 3rd and 7th of a chord define a chord's function and quality. In some blues styles, you can play solely a combination of roots, 3rds and 7ths for your left-hand accompaniment. It's necessary to be very familiar with the locations of the 3rds and 7ths in every key so you can use them easily for your blues progressions.

If you are playing with a bass player, you can play just the 3rd and 7th of each chord.

When playing solo, alternate between the root-7th and root-3rd.

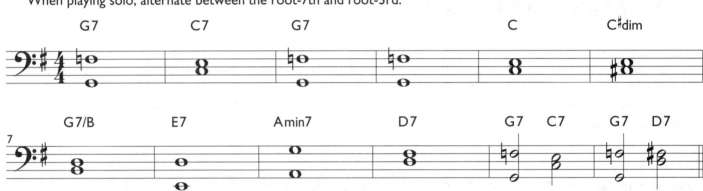

If your hand is big enough, you can play 10ths, one of the nicest sounds on the piano. A 10th is simply a 3rd with an extra octave inserted, giving it a more open sound. If you can't reach a 10th, fake it by rolling your hand quickly from the bottom note to the top note.

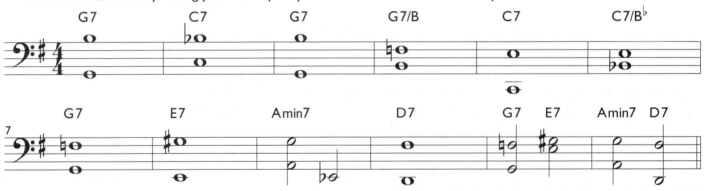

For a fuller sound, combine some walking lines with 3rds, 7ths and 10ths.

SWING FEEL

The blues often has a $\frac{12}{8}$ feel. The time signature is still $\frac{4}{4}$, but we take each quarter note and divide it into three. In other words, we play *eighth-note triplets*. Instead of playing two eighth notes per beat, we play three. Each bar then contains twelve triplet eighth-notes, which is why it is called $\frac{12}{8}$ feel, or triplet feel. It is also called *shuffle* feel.

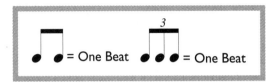

Let's get used to this feel by staying on the I chord, C Major, and playing eighth-note triplets with your right hand. Set your metronome to about 70 beats per minute and play three triplet eighth-notes on each click.

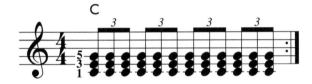

In this section, everything should be played with a swing feel unless marked "*Straight 8ths*."

In a typical shuffle bass pattern, we play triplets in the right hand. We also use the triplet feel in the left hand, but instead of writing triplets we write eighth notes with an indication that the eighths are *swung*. *Swinging the eighths* means that the first eighth note of each beat is held longer than the second.

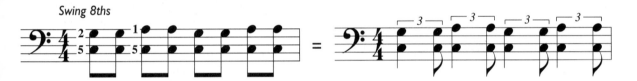

CYCLE OF 5THS

If we move from key to key at an interval of a perfect 5th, a sharp or flat will be added to the key signature each time we move. This movement is known as the *cycle of 5ths* (sometimes called the *circle* of 5ths). The cycle of 5ths forms the basis for most harmonic movement in popular music.

Since an inverted perfect 5th is a perfect 4th, the cycle of 5ths is sometimes called the cycle of 4ths. It's the same thing. Usually, when blues players think "cycle of 5ths," they are thinking counter-clockwise through the cycle—down by 5ths: C, F, B♭, E♭, etc.

The major key cycle is on the inside. The relative minor for each major key is outside the circle. Just like the major keys, the minor keys move up in 5ths as you add sharps, and down in 5ths as you add flats to the key signature.

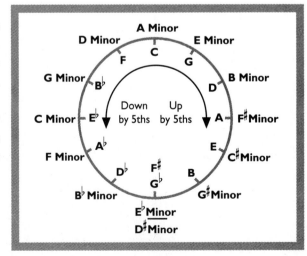

Let's review some different grooves. The definition of each feel will include the rhythmic fundamentals and a description of a typical bass part. Good keyboard parts are a result of complementing and accentuating these two things (or for solo piano, covering all three).

SHUFFLE

Your old friend the shuffle is marked by a strong triplet feel and a strong *backbeat*, which means the second and fourth beats of each bar are emphasized in the drum part. Shuffle bass patterns typically outline the chord, using a swing eighth rhythm.

SWING

The eighth notes in a swing feel are swung, but the triplet feel is not necessarily emphasized. The main emphasis is on the quarter note—four beats per bar played on the ride cymbal. The backbeat is present (the drummer plays the high-hat on 2 and 4) but not heavily emphasized. The bass generally walks:

SLOW $\frac{12}{8}$

Slow $\frac{12}{8}$ time is often written in $\frac{4}{4}$ and marked "triplet feel." Combine a triplet feel with a walking bass line and decrease the tempo as for a slow blues. The drummer emphasizes the quarter note and the triplet feel simultaneously.

THE TWO FEEL

A variation on swing. Instead of marking every quarter note, just 1 and 3 are emphasized (sounding like two beats per measure). Up-tempo swing tunes sometimes start out in a two feel. The bass plays simply—mainly on beats 1 and 3, alternating roots and chord tones.

SECOND-LINE GROOVE

Second line is the name given a rhythm the drummers in the second line of a New Orleans funeral procession played. The eighth-note feel is somewhere between straight and swung. The backbone of second-line groove is this dotted-quarter note pattern:

Bass parts for second-line grooves are based on the same pattern:

FUNK

The basic elements of funk grooves are straight eighths, a strong feeling of four and sixteenth note creativity. Having your sixteenth note rhythms together is an important part of being a competent modern blues and R&B player.

RHUMBA

Afro-Cuban in origin, rhumba inspired rhythms have been incorporated into both blues and jazz. The feel is similar to a second-line groove but the eighth notes are completely straight.

Once you understand the fundamentals of building a walking bass line (page 91) the next step is to develop your vocabulary. Knowing that there is more than one way to get from the I chord to the IV chord is one thing, but having it under your fingers is another. You need to practice different ways of getting through chord progressions so you don't always play exactly the same thing. As always, the best way to discover new sounds is by listening to recordings and transcribing what you hear. Here are some typical walking patterns to get you started.

SIX WAYS TO GET TO THE IV CHORD ON THE DOWNBEAT OF BAR 2

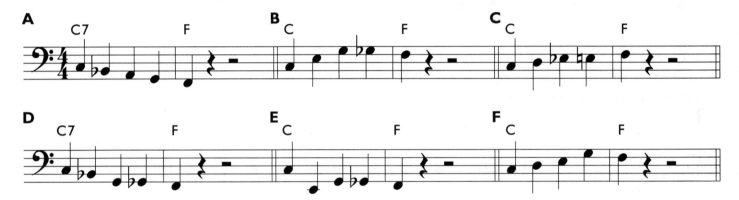

FOUR ROUTES BACK TO I

These assume that we used example A above to get to the IV chord.

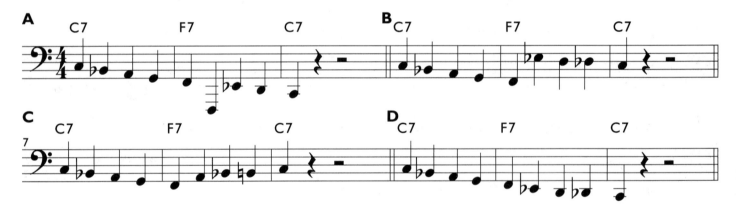

FOUR WAYS TO STAY ON I FOR EIGHT BEATS

Sometimes it seems tricky to stay on one chord for several bars. Each of these two-bar ideas can be repeated to fill four bars.

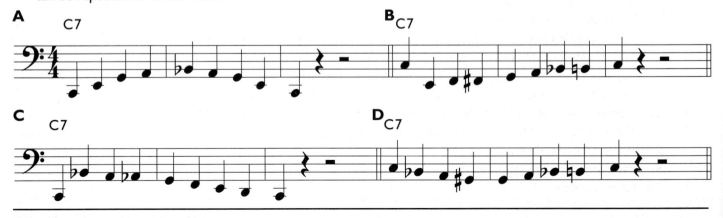

FOUR WAYS TO WALK THROUGH I-vi-ii-V

In Chapter 2 of the *Intermediate* section, you played an eight-bar blues called *Foolish Blues*. Here are two choruses of walking through the same blues progression. If you can recall the melody you learned, add it in your right hand.

Top Ten Tips for Walking Bass Lines

1. Play the root on beat one of the bar frequently. The 5th can work, too, or in the proper context, another chord tone such as the ♭7.
2. Think ahead—know where you are going.
3. Play primarily diatonic tones on the strong beats of the bar (beats 1 and 3). Reserve leading tones, passing tones or chromatic tones for the weak beats (beats 2 and 4).
4. Repeat notes (especially the root) if you wish.
5. Add occasional eighth notes if they make the line flow more smoothly.
6. Combine measures of walking with other typical bass patterns (boogie, shuffle, etc.).
7. Think of the bass line as a second melody.
8. Sing a bass line, then play it.
9. Vary your lines with octaves.
10. Keep it simple.

TREMOLOS

You've heard them—maybe you've already played them. If you haven't, you undoubtedly want to. *Tremolos* in the right hand, over a nice shuffle groove, are an essential ingredient in the blues sound. A tremolo is a rapid alternation between two notes. Sometimes blues players will call this a *roll*.

You can tremolo or roll between the root and the ♭3 of the key over almost the whole blues progression.

This is how tremolos or rolled notes are notated in the written music:

Tremolo on F and A♭ for five beats.

Tremolos are sometimes indicated like this:

CLUSTERS

A *cluster* is a group of notes that do not belong together as a chord but are played simultaneously. Often, it's just one of the notes that doesn't fit with the others. Below is an excerpt from a piece in the style of Otis Spann that was presented on page 50. The cluster (A♯, B, D) is hit as a chord and then arpeggiated.

GRACE NOTES/CRUSH TONES

When we play these figures off of triads, it's nice to add the ♭3 as a *grace note* preceding the 3rd. A grace note is a quick ornamental note played directly before the main note. It is sometimes called a *crush tone*. Some of us call this *bending the 3rd* because it sounds similar to a guitar player bending a note. It feels more natural in some keys than in others, depending upon where the black notes and white notes fall under your fingers. Here's how it works:

If the ♭3 is a black note, and the 3 is a white note, as in the keys of C, F or G, you can simply slide your 2nd finger from the ♭3 to the 3.

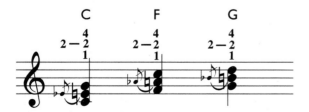

If the ♭3 is a white note, and the 3 is a black note, it's a little more awkward. Try playing the ♭3 with your 2nd finger and the 3 with your 3rd finger.

THE BASIC FORMS

TWELVE BARS

The classic twelve-bar blues form is as follows:

I	I	I	I	IV	IV	I	I	V	IV	I	I	‖
1	2	3	4	5	6	7	8	9	10	11	12	

A "quick four" in bar 2 is common, as is a half cadence (to V) in bar 12.

I	IV	I	I	IV	IV	I	I	V	IV	I	V	‖
1	2	3	4	5	6	7	8	9	10	11	12	

EIGHT BARS

Here are two common eight-bar progressions:

#1

I	i7	IV7	#ivdim	I	V7	I	V7	‖
1	2	3	4	5	6	7	8	

#2

I	I7	IV7	♭VII	I vi	ii V	I vi	ii V	‖
1	2	3	4	5	6	7	8	

SIXTEEN BARS

The classic sixteen-bar form appeared in Herbie Hancock's *Watermelon Man*.

I7	I7	I7	I7	IV7	IV7	I7	I7	
1	2	3	4	5	6	7	8	

V7	IV7	V7	IV7	V7	IV7 break	I7	I7	‖
9	10	11	12	13	14	15	16	

Another common sixteen-bar form has eight bars of I7, usually in stop-time or stop-time with a riff, followed by the last eight bars of a standard twelve-bar blues.

TURNAROUNDS

A *turnaround* is a musical figure used to lead you back to the top of the form. A turnaround usually ends on a V7 chord (a *half cadence*) since the dominant V7 chord leads back to the tonic.

BASIC TURNAROUNDS

Bass walks up from the 3rd of the I chord to the root of the V chord.

Bass walks down from the $\flat$7 of the I chord to the root of the V chord.

We can put these two *chromatic* (using notes outside the key) approaches together with two hands.

The word "chromatic" also implies movement in half-step increments, as in the *chromatic scale* (a twelve-note scale which includes all of the white notes and all of the black notes on the piano).

NEIGHBORING CHORDS

To play more involved turnarounds, you need to be familiar with the neighboring chords for the key. Neighboring chords lie a half step away from the chord you are approaching. A$\flat$7 is a neighboring chord to G7. D$\flat$7 is a neighboring chord to C7.

Here is a basic turnaround with a neighboring chord used to approach the V chord:

Endings have the opposite function of turnarounds. Instead of taking us back to the top of the form, they take us out. Interestingly, you can transform many turnaround figures into endings just by ending on a I chord instead of the V7.

Here's a familiar turnaround transformed into an ending:

This ending approaches the I chord from below:

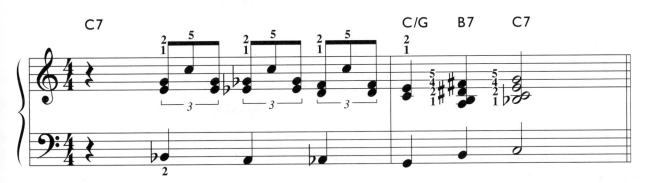

Not every blues starts with an introduction, but many of them do. As with every other aspect of the blues that we've talked about, there is some standard vocabulary to learn, as well as some room for creativity.

A common way to start a blues is to play a four-bar, V–IV–I intro with a little turnaround at the end.

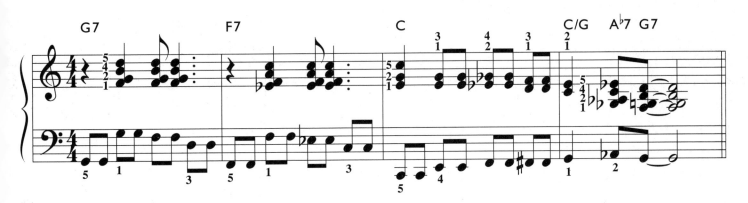

Improvising and Soloing

MOTIFS

Let's investigate what makes a musical line become an "old friend" that you're happy to hear every time you put on a CD. It's almost mystical, but the use of *motifs* (short rhythmic or melodic figures that recur) has a lot to do with it.

Every chorus of blues that you play should be unique. There are two ways to achieve this:

1) **Archival.** Many fine improvisers have learned hundreds of motifs from past masters which they use at appropriate moments.
2) **Spontaneous.** Creating new motifs.

This chapter will deal with spontaneous musical invention. Here are some ideas to help you make motifs that may qualify:

VERBAL

Remember, blues is lyric-based music. Use the rhythm, inflection and structure of language as a source for motifs. For instance, the phrase *"Don't you give me no lip!"* can give us this rhythm:

Track 2.1

> In this section, everything should be played wi[th] a swing feel unless marked *"Straight 8ths."*

The inflection may change depending on which word you want to emphasize. High notes or low notes both provide accentuation. Here's a way that idea can be applied to our motif:

Track 2.2

Structure comes when the line is inserted into verse form. We need to bear in mind that vocalists improvise with text using interjections, repetitions and new ideas.

NON-VERBAL

Motivic material can also be created non-verbally using patterns, numeric manipulation (for instance, using scale degrees based on a telephone number) and inspiration.

Collect motifs that you like in a manuscript notebook.

DEVELOPING A MOTIF

Once you have a motif, it's only a germ from which a melody can grow. Now we need to use it to tell a story. It must be developed. Here are some ideas to use:

The recommended tempo for all the examples on this page is ♩ = 104.

REPEAT

There are two good reasons for this: 1) so the listener will remember it; and 2), to give your solo shape. The **"golden rule of repetition"** has been used by all the greats, from Bach to Bo Diddley. The rule is the basis of the blues form: A A B. The first two repetitions are the same and the third starts the same but ends differently. In a solo, you can use this on a smaller scale. For example:

Track 3.1

SEQUENCE

Repeat the motif on a different scale degree. Remember the "golden rule of repetition!"

Track 3.2

INVERT

Turn it upside down.

Track 3.3

RETROGRADE

Play it backwards. Jimmy Hendrix perfected this to the degree that it sounded like a tape being played backwards. Okay—so it's a little esoteric. But it works!

Track 3.4

SHIFTED RHYTHM

Start the motif in a different place in the bar.

Track 3.5

NOTE:
An exception to the *"golden rule of repetition"* is that, after five or six repetitions, the interest curve rises. This is common practice in the blues and makes a great climax.

FRAGMENT

Cut and paste. Use little pieces of the motif to make a larger shape. Stretch it, compress it, make it "stutter."

Track 3.6

Not everything you play will be a motif. Between statements of motifs, the first option is to rest. Just let the rhythm section, or your left hand, maintain the pulse, feel and texture. This is called using *space*. A second option is to play a groove figure—anything from short quarter notes in the style of Freddy Green to a funk-motor figure or Latin *guajeo* (dance rhythm)—in other words, join the rhythm section momentarily.

A third option is to use some kind of "connective tissue:" sweep, a glissando, scale or pattern of any length leading into the beginning of the motif.

Or, try a "trail-off" growing out of the end of the motif.

Also, for a more sophisticated, higher intensity (and more jazz oriented) format, motivic material can be connected by scales, patterns and freely invented material.

Some Thoughts

Make the motion of your line balanced and logical. Don't end on the tonic ("1" of the scale) until the end of the solo, if you must at all. Ending phrases with a leap or scale segment (final note staccato as in example 11) leaves the listener anticipating the next phrase.

THE DOUBLE MELODIC LINE AND ITS USES

For added interest and a bigger, more complex sound, try thinking of your right hand as playing a double melodic line (two melodies at once).

The recommended tempo for all the examples on this page is ♩ = 112.

REITERATED PEDAL TONE

A *pedal tone* is a sustained or continuously repeated tone.

13 Track 5.1

Example 13 combines this pedal tone: …and this melody:

14 Track 5.2

RUDIMENTAL DRUMMING STRUCTURES

Here's one based on a *paradiddle* (a drum rudiment where strokes alternated as follows: RLRR LRLL).

R = Right
L = Left

15 Track 5.3

Example 15 combines this: and this:

16 Track 5.4

CALL AND RESPONSE

Call and response with the hand jumping from one register to another gives the effect of more than one player. Example 17 has a riff alternating with improvisation.

17 Track 5.5

The following patterns are useful for building motifs and connective tissue. Experiment and find personal ways of doing each of these in the chromatic, diatonic and blues scales, ascending and descending and in all keys. Also, you should invent many patterns of your own.

The recommend
tempo for all t
examples on th
page is ♩ = 144.

Diads sequenced up the scales.

18
Track 6.1

Triads

19
Track 6.2

Four-Note Sequence

20
Track 6.3

Broken 3rds

21
Track 6.4

Broken 4ths

22
Track 6.5

A Word About Patterns:

Don't let them become mechanical. Vary them by superimposing unusual rhythms, inserting rests, repeated notes and repeating fragments.

PERMUTATIONS

Any group of notes can be put through *permutations* (re-orderings) and then applied to a scale. In the first measure of example 23, for instance, a three-note motif including C (1), E♭ (♭3) and F (4) of the C Minor Pentatonic scale is put through six permutations in a measure of $\frac{6}{4}$ time. The measure starts on C (1). In the second measure, all six permutations are repeated, this time starting on the next note in the C Minor Pentatonic scale, E♭ (♭3). If we think of the six permutations as one line, then the second measure is a sequence of the first. We can think of the second measure as being in the 2nd Mode of the minor pentatonic scale (you can think of any scale as having modes). Whew! Then, there is a third repetition on the 3rd Mode. This is an excellent exercise for developing facility with any scale or set of chord tones.

In the next example, put these fingerings, or modes of the C Pentatonic scale, through the same permutations as in example 23.

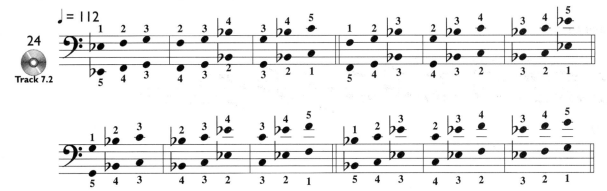

The figure in example 25 is good for another effect: the *flurry*. A flurry is a group of fast notes that makes the audience think, "Wow, this person can play!" The three-note permutations from example 23 are put through the blues scale, but the root rises chromatically on each group of three! If this makes your brain hurt, it's okay. Just spend some time gazing at examples 23 and 25 and it'll click eventually.

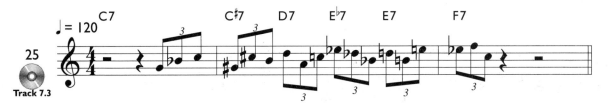

Here's another example of a flurry using two, two-note units (F and G♭; F and E):

Hopefully, the ideas below will fire your imagination. They also show how really cool stuff can come from a simple idea. Think of these as "devices" which you should have in your "bag."

Repeated tone followed by scale (or arpeggio):

27 Track 8.1

Repeated tone as an arrival point of arpeggio (or scale):

28 Track 8.2

Leap followed by scale in opposite direction:

29 Track 8.3

Embellishments on successive chord or scale tones:

30 Track 8.4

Two alternating tones followed by a leap:

31 Track 8.5

Fingers Aflame, on the next page, has two choruses using some of these ideas.

Exercise:

Take two or three of these ideas and to play a continuous line alternating th for as long as possible.

---

216 Mastering Blues Keyboard

FINGERS AFLAME

Listeners hear a melody as a band of sound. It can be a thin band of sound (single note line) or a thicker band of sound. It can be made thicker by harmonizing, or duplicating, the line with a specific interval in parallel motion. On page 116, you learned a classic blues lick with notes harmonized in 3rds mid-way through.

This kind of harmonization of a line, or portions of a line, creates interest by varying the color of the line, underscoring important motivic ideas, distinguishing separate voices in hockets or "call and response" structures, or just by adding bright highlights in unexpected places.

Try using longer passages in 3rds.

Example 34 uses 4ths.

Harmonizing in 6ths makes a very sweet sound.

Octaves are effective, too.

To make the harmonic density of your moving lines even wider, duplicate them in 3rds, 6ths and 4ths at the same time. That brings us to our next topic, *block voicing*.

BLOCK VOICING

To get the maximum intricacy and variety of color and texture in your playing, imitate the big band sound. The main stylistic device you should adopt is saxophone-section-type block voicing. Here some ways you can do this:

Single Hand—Triadic

> The recommended tempo for all the examples on this page is ♩ = 104.

Single Hand—Added Note or 7th Chord Voicings

Two Hands Locked (George Shearing's innovation)

Two Hands Harmonized at the Octave

"Poor Man's Block Voicing"—Right-Hand Melody in Octaves with the Left-Hand Chord Voicing Played in Rhythmic Unison

Here is a composition imitating a big band and demonstrating some of these types of block voicing. The chords in the last two measures require the reach of a 10th. If this is impractical for you, roll the chords.

THE INCREDIBLE EXPANDING RIFF

CHAPTER 3

Variety in Turnarounds and Progressions

TRITONE SUBSTITUTION

Substituting one chord for another is one of the most important tools we have for varying a blues progression. One of the most popular substitutions is the *tritone substitution*. Any dominant 7th chord can be replaced with another dominant 7th chord whose root is three whole steps—a tritone—away. This works because the 3rd and the 7th of any dominant 7th chord are also the 7th and 3rd, respectively, of the dominant 7th chord a tritone away.   For instance, the 3rd of a C7 chord is E. The 7th of the G♭7 chord is F♭, the enharmonic equivalent of E. The 7th of the C7 is B♭, which is also the 3rd of the G♭7.

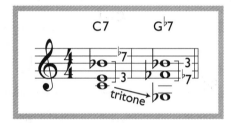

So, to make your blues progression more interesting, the dominant 7th chord on V can be replaced by a dominant 7th chord on the ♭2 (you learned an ending like this in the *Intermediate* section). And, in any cycle of 5ths progression of dominant chords, such as vi-ii-I, any chord can be replaced by its tritone substitute.

We can apply this to the I-vi-ii-V turnaround. Below is a chart showing the possibilities.

TABLE OF TRITONE SUBSTITUTIONS FOR I-vi-ii-V IN C			
I	**vi**	**ii**	**V**
C	A7	D7	G7
C	A7	A♭7	G7
C	A7	A♭7	D♭7
C	A7	D7	D♭7
C	E♭7	D7	G7
C	E♭7	D7	D♭7
C	E♭7	A♭7	G7
C	E♭7	A♭7	D♭7

Most of these should sound familiar to you since they are frequently used. Many other variations are possible.

Exercise:

Try: 1) using two changes per measure by including substitutions;
    2) starting the cycle of 5ths in a different place than vi;
    3) putting a iimin7 chord before any V7 chord;
    4) inserting root movement of a 3rd or 2nd anywhere in a cycle of 5ths progression.
These procedures should help you invent new chord progressions for some time to come.

The table below shows common substitutions used in a twelve-bar blues. These are by no means all the possibilities, but they'll get you started on your own path to discovering others. The chart is divided into twelve equal sections, each one representing a bar of the twelve-bar blues. There are four beats per bar. Except where noted, two chords in a bar means there are two beats per chord, four chords means one beat per chord.

SUBSTITUTIONS FOR THE TWELVE-BAR BLUES

C7-I			
C7 G♭7	F7	C7	Gmin7 C7
	F7 F#dim7		C7 G♭7
C	Bmin7♭5 E7	Amin7 D7	Gmin7 G♭7
	E7	F7 F#dim	Gmin7 C7
	E7	A7	D7 G7 Gmin7 C7
C7 F7	B♭7 E♭7	A♭7 D♭7	F#7 B7

F7-IV		C7-I	
	F#dim		A7
	B♭7		E♭7
	B♭7 Bdim		E♭m7 A♭m7
			Am7♭5 D7
		C7 B7	B♭7 A7
		C7 F7	B♭7 E♭7
		C7 B7	E7 E♭7
F7 B♭7	E♭7 D7 D♭7	C7 F7	B♭7 E♭7

G7-V	F7-IV	C7-I	G7-V
Dmin7	G7		A♭min7 D♭7
Dmin7 G7		B♭min7 E♭7	D7 G7
	Cmin7 F7	A7	A♭7 G7
	A♭7 G7	B♭7	F F#dim
	Dmin7♭5 G7	C7/E	F B♭7
		C7/E	
A7 D7	A♭7 D♭7	C G7*	G7

*This chord falls on the second beat of the bar.

Two closing thoughts:

1) Notice how the blues scale notes (G, B♭, C, E♭) become more colorful over the G♭7 chord, which is the tritone substitution for the tonic chord. They become ♭9 (G or A♭♭), 3 (B♭), #11 (C) and 13 (E♭).

2) On an historical note, Art Tatum invented new chord progressions as he was improvising —something to work towards.

CHAPTER 4

Multiple Functions of the Hands and Independence

In Chapter 2 we dealt briefly with the double melodic line as a way of increasing interest and complexity. In this chapter, we'll look at some devices for more sophisticated comping. First, let's expand on a classic blues lick you learned in the *Intermediate* section, where the tonic is sustained against a simple motif.

In this section, everything should be played with a swing feel unless marked "*Straight 8ths*."

Sustaining the 6th can also work in this structure.

Try it with the 3rd.

It can also work with one of any two adjacent 3rds in any chord. For example, here's the concept applied in four ways through a C9 chord:

From supporting a motif with a single note, we move to sustaining one note and, with the same hand, using the other notes in the chord to play time or comp.

Similarly, we can play a melody or repeated single note with the thumb while the other fingers comp or play a bass line.

A more complex strategy would be "tiling the plane" with interlocking rudimental patterns. For instance, take this pattern:

Combine it with this one, which is really just the inversion of the first:

You get something like this:

There is also an important multiple function for the left hand. We can alternate between a bass line and chordal accompaniment.

Here is an example in the style of New Orleans blues:

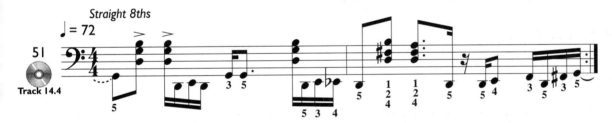

Here's an example of the same technique, but this time in a Rhythm and Blues (R&B) context:

Independence is the ability to simultaneously play completely different things in each hand. In group situations, if you have good independence you can add another layer of texture to the overall sound. This is also a very useful thing when you are playing solo. Here are a series of exercises that, if used as prescribed, will allow you to learn to improvise freely over any bass line or ostinato (an accompaniment figure that is repeated).

Step 1. Practice the bass line with your metronome until it is completely comfortable and doesn't require all of your attention.

Step 2. As you play the bass line in the left hand, play an eighth-note chord tone in the right hand (root or 5th are good choices) on the downbeat. Do this eight times. Then, strike the right-hand note on the "&" of "1" eight times. Then move on to the "2," etc. Do this on every eighth-note pulse in the bar. Be sure your metronome is still on, set to a slow tempo.

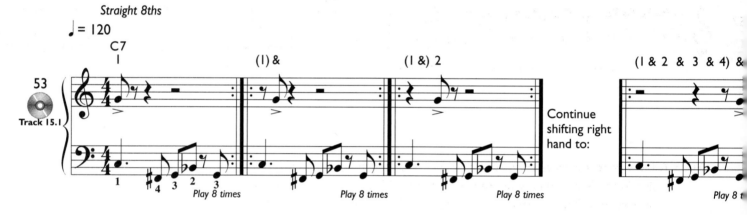

Step 3. Now, hit on every eighth with the right hand while repeating the bass line in the left. Do this until it is comfortable.

Step 4. Now alternate your right-hand pitch with its upper neighboring tone in the scale until it flows. For now, let's assume we're using the G Dorian scale, because it works well over the bass.

Step 5. Then proceed to the next scale degree and alternate that with your starting pitch. Repeat this step with all the degrees of the scale between your starting pitch and the next octave.

Step 6. Repeat Steps 4 and 5, this time starting with a lower neighbor tone descending through the scale from there.

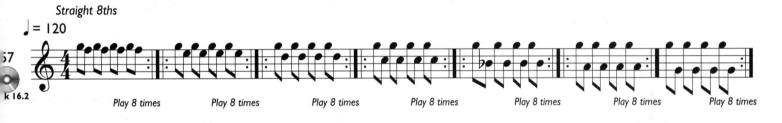

Step 7. Now repeat a three-note scale segment in the right hand while playing the bass line in the left. When you are comfortable with this, play the entire scale up to the interval of a 9th and back again, using a 1-2-3 thumb-under fingering. Repeat until secure.

Step 8. Now attempt simple right-hand patterns (refer to page 214 and your own notebook) over the bass line, still using eighth notes. Start with simple patterns (broken 3rds, broken 4ths, etc.) and work towards more complex and more *syncopated* patterns. Practice syncopation on every beat in the bar or bars.

IMPROVISING YOUR WALKING BASS LINES

Like any proficient bass player, when playing left hand (or organ pedal) walking bass lines, you should be able to play an interesting new line every chorus. Here are some helpful things to bear in mind:

WALKING BASS CONSIDERATIONS

1. The easiest way to make a walking bass line is to use these scale degrees:
   Ascending—1-2-#2-3
   Descending—8-7-6-5.

   Both allow an easy route away from or towards the tonic.

2. If your chord progression root is moving up a 4th, it is only necessary to make sure the 7th degree in your line agrees with the 7th of the first chord.

3. The first chord can be either major or minor, since #2 is the same as ♭3 and 3 can be a chromatic passing tone leading to the root of the next chord.

4. On a minor chord where the root movement is not a 4th, you can use 1-#1-2-♭3.

♩ = 126

59 Track 17.1

SOME OTHER POSSIBILITIES

CHORDAL OUTLINE

When outlining triads, repeat one note to get a four-beat bar. With 7th chords, avoid the 7th at the end of the bar unless:

1. it's a leading tone to the next root; or
2. the next chord is being played in 1st inversion (with the 3rd in the bass).

♩ = 126

60 Track 17.2

ANY COMBINATION OF OCTAVES AND 5THS

Also octaves and 5ths with lower chromatic neighboring tones.

Track 18.1

CHORDAL OUTLINE WITH PASSING TONES

You can use actual passing tones to connect the chord tones (all stepwise motion) or skip up or down to non-chord tones (as long as they resolve to chord tones).

Track 18.2

FLAMS

Keep your bass line alive and interesting by inserting occasional eighth notes, triplet eighths, and, most importantly, *flams*. The flam (grace note) can be almost anything. Some possibilities include:

> The previous bass note
> The same pitch as the bass note
> Any chordal tone, an out of the key escape tone
> A right-hand chord or
> Part of a chord in either hand
> Anything else you can think of!

Below are some examples of *flams*. Notice that they can be written either as grace notes or as actual rhythms. They can even include multiple notes. Let these examples spur your imagination, then come up with some of your own. Have fun!

Track 18.3

> *Exercise:*
>
> Apply each walking bass device on pages 228 and 229 to all the tunes with walking bass lines in the last few chapters. Try them with pairs of chords, particularly ii7 – V7, and cycle of 5ths progressions. Cozy-up to this area of study—spend some time with it every day.

> **TIP:**
>
> To sound more "bass-like," play written bass lines down an octave whenever possible.

In Chapter 4 of the *Intermediate* section, you were introduced to the idea of creating bass lines by mixing walking lines with other devices, such as shuffle patterns. Here's an example of this kind of line:

Your solo playing will be much more interesting if, on some tunes, you expand on this idea and alternate lines that are even more diverse. Masters of this technique include Earl Hines, Meade Lux Lewis, Errol Garner and Art Tatum. In a single chorus, you might alternate a few bars of a groove figure with:

A bar or two of stop time (left hand silent or sustaining the chord – right hand in flight)
A melodic statement (or response) in octaves
A *hammered* (struck repeatedly) interval root and 5th broken up by chords
A broken octave pedal point
A swirling chromatic scale connecting one root to the next
A vigorous trill
Marcato (accented) left-hand chords
Etc.!

*The legendary and innovative **Earl "Fatha" Hines**, born in 1903, spent the better part of the 20th century at the top of the jazz piano heap.*

The possibilities are endless. Select or invent your own vocabulary of accompaniments, then set up your own exercises to develop this facility. Below is a very free application of this concept.

CRAZY QUILT

Here is a composition using a New Orleans-style, multi-function left-hand part which gives the effect of repeated chords and a bass line in the left hand. *Your Indigo Purgatory* is in the style of the changes to *My Blue Heaven*. If you need to, roll the 10ths.

YOUR INDIGO PURGATORY

Here is another New Orleans-style, multi-function left-hand figure in the style of James Booker. The effect here is a free bass line and repeated chords set in a more syncopated rhythm.

Mac Rebennack soaked up the music of great New Orleans players like Professor Longhair, Fats Domino, Huey 'Piano' Smith and Allan Toussaint, and draped himself in the voodoo legends and symbolism of his city to become **Dr. John the Night Tripper**. His show introduced the psychedelic movement to New Orleans sounds and established him as a hip R&B artist with a Delta twist. He played guitar as a teenager but got shot in the hand, losing the use of his left index finger. Then James Booker helped him with his organ playing and he played his first keyboard gigs. Dr. John went on to work as a solo pianist, composer, singer, psychedelic rock star and producer.

MORE ABOUT STRIDE

The recommended tempo for all the examples on this page is ♩ = 100.

In the *Intermediate* section, you learned the basics of stride: the left hand alternates between bass notes on beats 1 and 3 and a chord voicing on the backbeat (beats 2 and 4 of the bar). This was the style as developed by James P. Johnson. Fats Waller, who roomed with Johnson briefly when he was young, added a major innovation. Critics called what Waller was doing a "fist full of keys" approach to the piano. Instead of single bass notes on beats 1 and 3, he would play a 5th, 10th or big open position chord.

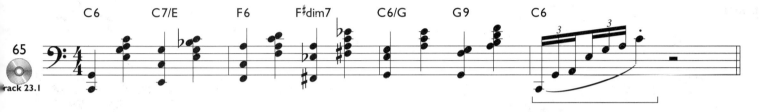

Instead of using single-note walking lines to connect stride patterns, Waller would play 10ths or even open position 7th chords.

The sound of stride played well is massive, virtuosic and very entertaining. It is also a specialty that takes many long hours of practice to really master. If you are inclined, do the exercises below around the cycle of 5ths. Start very slowly. It is essential that you learn them by feel. Do them until you can play them with your eyes closed or your hands covered with a light cloth.

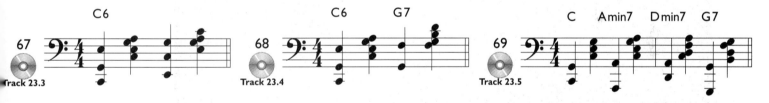

In the event that your time for practicing such things is limited, here are some thoughts about imitating the stride sound. First, use broken, open or closed position left-hand voicings. You will sacrifice mass and power, but you can maintain the motion and idea of stride. Second, using the multi-function ideas from pages 224 and 225, you can put the off beats in the lower part of the right hand, the upper part of the left hand, or both together. Also, in a difficult situation, simply playing a chord voicing on the appropriate melody note in the right hand can preserve the stride motion.

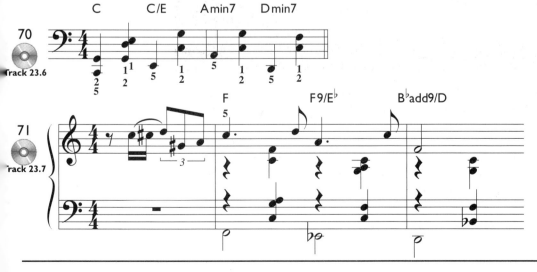

Here is a piece using stride (some real, some not so real) and some alternation of bass figures in the style of Art Tatum. Note the rhythm in measure 7. It's a quarter-note triplet subdivided into 16ths. Think of three quarters in the time of two, then subdivide.

Track 24

GOD WAS IN THE HOUSE

CHAPTER 5

Blues Organ

When we talk about the organ in blues, R&B, gospel are referring primarily to the Hammond B-3. There is nothing really comparable to the B-3 sound. Although often imitated, nothing duplicates the sound of the B-3 with a Leslie speaker, and the history and development of Blues organ parallels the integration of the Hammond B-3 into popular music.

B-3 owners are an exclusive club. Besides an initial outlay of up to $8,000 for a mint condition organ with Leslie speaker, the organs are expensive to maintain, and, at more than 400 pounds for the organ plus 150 pounds for the Leslie, they are difficult to move. Since production of the original B-3 was discontinued in 1974, parts and service can be difficult to obtain. However, many players and listeners consider these challenges a small price to pay. In spite of advances in digital sampling keyboards, even a large sample library can't begin to equal the rainbow of sounds that a great B-3 player like Booker T. Jones can create as he plays.

The mighty Hammond B-3

From the beginning, organs have been intended to put all the sounds of the orchestra or band at the fingertips of a single player. The B-3 was originally intended as an alternative to pipe organs in churches and for use as an instrument in the home. The Leslie speaker, with its rotating horn and drum, was designed to imitate the sound of the pipe organ with pitches emanating from different pipes around the hall. The closest thing to a jazz big band is a "Texas organ trio"—a guitarist or saxophonist and a drummer fleshing out a keyboard player's pedal or left-hand bass, comping and soloing.

Rotating "tone wheels," each of which has from two to one-hundred-ninety-two notched teeth, generates the sound of a Hammond organ. As they turn, the notches create a fluctuation in a coil wound around a permanent magnet. A wheel with a higher number of notches produces a higher pitch. When the keys make contact, there is an audible click. While this sound was not popular in churches and homes, it gave an articulated attack that was much prized by players of rhythmic, driving music.

Some of the early Hammond organ players were Fats Waller, Count Basie and Wild Bill Davis. Some other noted players are Shirley Scott, Jack McDuff, Jackie Davis, Billy Preston, Dr. Lonnie Smith, Rosemary Bailey, John Patton, Milt Buchner, Joe Bucci, Jimmy McGriff, John Medeski (of Medeski, Martin & Wood), Joey DeFrancesco and, of course, the great Jimmy Smith. Collecting and studying recordings of this abbreviated list will give you a good start on developing a concept of what organ should sound like in a blues and jazz context.

Owners and prospective owners of Hammond organs are referred to the excellent book by Mark Vail, *The Hammond Organ – Beauty and the B,* published by Miller Freeman, United News and Media Publications, which treats history, workings and operating information in exhaustive detail.

A QUICK GUIDE TO OPERATING THE B-3

Here is the procedure for turning the organ on:

1. Put the *start switch* to the "on" position.

2. When the sound changes, release the start switch and turn on the *run switch*.

3. Give it time to warm up. Oil from two small reservoirs is actually working its way through the organ's moving parts.

The bottom octave of each of the two *manuals* (a manual is a keyboard—the B-3 has two) has the colors of the keys reversed. These are not notes. They are *presets*. A preset is a combination of settings used to get a particular sound. These can be achieved with one touch of a preset key.

Above the upper manual are two sets of *drawbars* arranged in four groups of nine each. Each drawbar mixes in a specific *overtone* from the lowest (corresponding to a sixteen-foot organ pipe) to the highest (corresponding to a one-foot organ pipe). An overtone is a *harmonic*—a lesser, higher tone that accompanies each *fundamental* tone. Each group of nine drawbars is color-coded in white, black and brown. When pushed all the way in, a drawbar does not affect the sound. If it is pulled out to "8," it produces its maximum effect. The specific combination of overtones is what creates familiar and new timbers. Manipulating these drawbars with one hand while you play with the other hand allows you to continuously vary your sound.

One of the features the Hammond is most famous for is the triggered percussion effect. This is a percussive sound that accompanies the attack of a note. It is found on the upper manual only. Four switches control this effect:

1. On/Off switch

2. Volume (normal and soft)

3. Decay time (fast or slow)

4. Two choices for the pitch of the harmonic above the note
   • the octave, which is called "second"
   • an octave and a 5th, which is called "third"

To trigger the percussion effect on every note, it is necessary to play staccato. Otherwise, only the first note of a phrase will have percussion added to it.

Post 1945 Hammonds have a four-position switch that gives three speeds of vibrato and an "Off" setting. Later models have a chorus effect added with three position labels: C1, C2 and C3.

GETTING STARTED WITH DRAWBAR SETTINGS

A good place to start for a bass sound is the 16' (sixteen foot, as in a sixteen foot organ pipe) drawbar on 8, $5^{1}/_{3}$' on 2, 8' on 8. Experiment with coloring the sound by using some of the higher drawbars.

Most players start with the first three or four drawbars out and percussion on either setting. To increase the sound as you play additional choruses, try pulling out the highest drawbars more in each successive chorus. Or, move from high drawbars to low drawbars. By adding drawbars, you can swell the sound very similarly to what you can do with the volume pedal. When comping, avoid overpowering the soloist by not using the lowest drawbars. The Hammond Organ Company's manual advised against ever pulling all the drawbars all the way out. But the expression "pulling out all the stops" originated with organ players, and most players confess to having committed this sin at some time to compete with loud bands.

Individual drawbar settings are often jealously guarded secrets. *Hammond Organ – Beauty in the B* by Mark Vail lists the configurations of many famous organists.

IMPLICATIONS OF ORGAN KEYBOARD ACTION

Organ differs from piano in that the keys require less force to play. This means that *glissandos* (rapid scales played by sliding fingers over the keys) are much easier on organ. While piano glisses have to be done with the back of the 3rd finger fingernail or the thumb nail, organists can use almost any part of the finger or thumb and even the palms of their hands. These variations change the sound of the glissando and are a part of the B-3 vocabulary. Because of the ease with which they can be played, you can be very fanciful and imaginative in their use.

Some things organists can do are:

> Multiple glisses hand over hand.
>
> Glissandos in contrary motion (one hand going up and one hand going down simultaneously).
>
> Climbing or falling zigzags with a single hand or changing hands with the changes of direction.
>
> Grand sweeps to the beginning of a motif.
>
> Fall-offs at the end of a phrase.
>
> Sags (a gliss down from a note or chord of any size, and then up again returning to the same note or chord).
>
> Short upward or downward glisses on every note of a scale or arpeggiated passage.

To make the note or chord at the end of an adventurous gliss more secure, have the other hand play the end note of the gliss, and put it in position as you gliss with the other hand.

A second benefit of easy keyboard action is speed. Jimmy Smith is probably one of the fastest musicians who ever lived. This is due to both his amazing technique and, in some part, to the instrument he chose to play. Organ keys return to position very quickly which allows for rapid reiteration of notes and chords. This makes trills very easy. More so than with piano, an organist can imitate the sounds of hand drums or even a trap set by using rudimental rhythm patterns between hands or fingers.

When soloing, think of your right hand as a horn player. The left hand is then free to vary the sound by changing drawbar settings, vibrato and chorus. Because organ pitches sustain indefinitely, you can use long notes that would just die away if you were playing piano. A long note at the peak of a line, with a scale leading into it and out of it, makes a good climax.

> In this section, everything should be played with a swing feel unless marked "Straight 8ths."

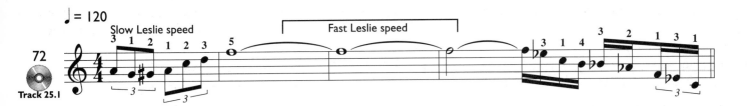

For a heavier climax, use an *inverted pedal point* (a high note held as the harmony changes underneath) and end with a descending scale or gliss.

Don't forget to let your lines breathe in a human manner so that listeners can digest what you play phrase by phrase. This will also give the listener a rest from the color of the instrument, however briefly, so they won't tire of the sound as quickly. Because there is no sustain pedal, as there is on the piano, it is good to occasionally hold a note or notes in the line as discussed in Chapter 4 with the multiple function of the hand exercises.

When creating backgrounds, the organ's sustain allows you to imitate the string orchestra. For harmonic continuity, keep your voicings in this register: F below middle C to G above middle C.

The recommended tempo for all examples on this page is ♩ = 72.

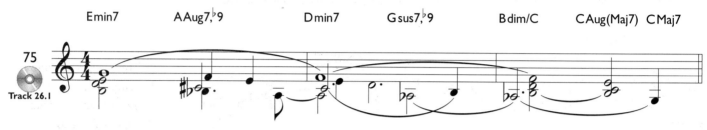

Think of each note as an individual voice or section of the string orchestra. Embellish a note before it moves.

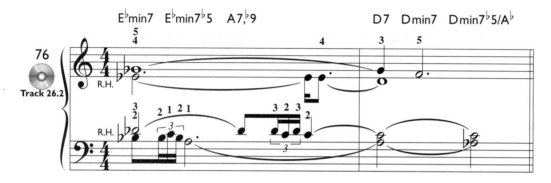

When a note moves more than a step, connect it to the following pitch with a chromatic or diatonic scale.

Sustain some notes of a chord and simultaneously tremolo others.

These devices will make listeners aware of single voices as they would be with real strings. Be sure to taper your chords with the swell pedal or drawbar registration to emulate one of the major characteristics of live strings. Splitting string sounds between the manuals will also give your strings sound more depth.

Descant-style (a high part above the melody) upper-register lines in single notes, or harmonized in parallel 3rds, 6ths or 10ths can be very effective. Keep the drawbar registration light and use chorus, vibrato and reverb to enhance the string-like effect.

For riffing and punch chords, think brass. Big sounds, heavy registration, edgy sounds, short note punctuations and interjections, two-handed tremolos in the style of the Basie Band's are the vocabulary to draw on here. This is a good time to review the block voicing material in Chapter 2.

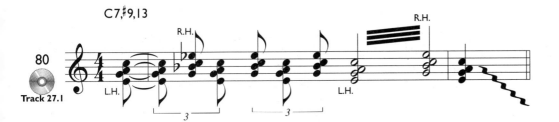

> The recommended tempo for all the examples on this page is $\downarrow$ = 120.

A very effective device to use in conjunction with the percussion feature, is *clipping*. Hit a full chord or even a diatonic cluster (all the notes in a scale segment played simultaneously) and quickly release all but one or two notes.

The held notes can merely last longer than the rest of the chord or can be the beginning of the next line.

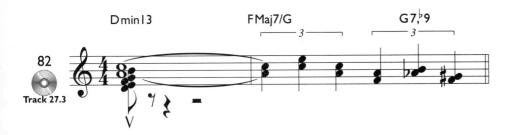

As with any serious musical study, you must acquaint yourself with the body of work that has accumulated for the instrument. Collect CD's, records and tapes from the masters mentioned in this chapter and listen, listen, listen, so you will begin the lifelong process of assimilating their achievements.

CHAPTER 6

Rhythm Section Playing, Comping and Grooving

PLAYING IN A BAND

The more people in the band, the less you play. Here are some other good rules of thumb:

- Just because you can play the bass line with the bass player doesn't mean you should.
- If both you and the guitarist comp at the same time, the end result will be rigid and very possibly rhythmically and harmonically cluttered (unless you are both extremely sensitive and ear training experts).
- Doubling any part of a drum figure may occasionally be desirable as a coloristic effect but, unless you give it your undivided attention, chances are good it will lack precision and obscure the pulse.
- An amplified keyboard (organ, synthesizer or piano), unless used judiciously, can cloud the air around any horn section.
- Most importantly, don't play all the time. This would make the band monochromatic. Listeners never have a chance to miss you if you're always in their faces!

It can be very effective to duplicate one or two notes of a bass line and occasionally double the bass in an ensemble passage when no one is soloing. Don't be heavy-handed about this. If the bass player glares at you, you should probably cease and desist. For the sake of clarity, it is best to mostly stay out of the bass player's register. This will also avoid tuning problems, particularly if the bassist is playing string bass or fretless bass guitar. Your left hand voicing in the comping register (F below middle C to G above middle C) and a fat bass note make a complete picture. Nothing else is necessary.

Two instruments comping simultaneously is usually wasted color. With few exceptions, the arranger's rule is "doubled notes are wasted notes." When working with another keyboard player or guitarist, trade off comping and filling functions or just take turns resting. A single comper allows for more rapid and effective responses to what the soloist is doing. If you stay alert, you and your fellow compers can develop the empathy to make fascinating and unpredictable changes in function and orchestration without stepping on each other's toes.

In a small group format, it is often appropriate to double the backbeat. In larger groups, it becomes more rare. It is more effective to add another unique rhythmic layer. A high keyboard pitch could, for instance, play a Latin rhythm (read about the *clavé rhythm* in Chapter 8). Or one could play a repeated figure in staccato, quarter-note triplets (in the mid-range and omitting the first beat) to add an unobtrusive layer. Always strive for a carefully balanced volume. Let taste and reserve be your guides.

If you double the horn section, your rhythmic precision (attacks and durations) as well as your volume level must be at the same level of perfection that horn players generally demand of themselves. Responses to horn riffs and punches are safer and more entertaining to hear. Other strategies are sweeps into, trail-offs from and flams before horn section figures. Again, don't overdo it.

Don't forget the comper's prime directive: ***make the soloist sound great and don't get in the way***. All the things you do to create a climax in your own solos can be used when comping. If you can insert the right device at the right moment at the right volume to put the soloist over the top, you will be in demand.

Feel, or groove, comes from maintaining a steady, predictable pulse and then tugging or pulling against that pulse. *Laying back* (playing slightly behind each beat) creates a relaxed feel, and playing on the front part of the beat creates an edgy and exuberant feel. The rhythm section creates one tonal/rhythmic plane and the soloist creates a second. The friction between these two generates groove. As the two move in tandem, sharing the same pulse, the soloist is free to break formation by playing one or more of the following:

Cross rhythms (rhythms with accents that do not coincide with those of the rhythm section).

> In this section, everything should be played with a swing feel unless marked "*Straight 8ths.*"

Hemiolas (making rhythmic groupings that have a different downbeat than the band's meter, such as groups of three in common time, or, as in this case, something more unusual, such as groups of seven notes in common time).

Polyrhythms (two completely different tempos played simultaneously—the soloist plays a different rhythm/tempo than the rhythm section). Example 85 shows a 5 against 2 rhythm (5:2) in $\frac{3}{4}$ time.

All of these devices allow the soloist to pull the listener away from the rhythm section's pulse and replace it momentarily with another. This creates tension which is released when the soloist returns to the rhythm section's pulse. The simplest illustration of this principle is the well-worn device of playing a series of off-beat quarter notes. Listeners attempting to track the beat are pulled to the off-beats with the soloist and, whether or not they can keep their toes tapping on the beat, they recognize the original pulse when the off-beats stop. This game is very entertaining.

VOCAL ACCOMPANIMENT IN A DUO FORMAT

For many pianists, accompanying a good singer is one of their favorite activities. The challenge of supplying the bass line, changes, fills and a workable musical conception is the source of the thrill. In addition to all we have discussed about comping behind a soloist, ideally the complete accompanist should be flexible enough to play well in all keys. They should also know the singer's voice well enough to choose keys that exploit the tonal colors of its various registers. Positioning a critical note exactly on the singer's *break* between chest voice and head voice can move the performance from "ho-hum" to gut wrenching. Moving a low passage down a step, or even a half step, can sometimes put enough gravel in the voice to add an aura of sincerity to a confession of love or lust.

Playing behind a melody with words opens up the possibility of *tone painting*. The vocal literature of the blues is replete with moaning train whistles, visits to honky tonks and speakeasies, police sirens heralding unjustified searches and arrests, various states and flavors of inebriation and "Amen" responses to preaching. All these are obvious and traditional situations where a few well chosen notes can be very evocative. Err on the side of subtlety. Better to be subliminal than corny.

To make your fills a seamless part of your accompaniment, begin the line from a unison with a vocal note or comping figure. Continue the directional motion of the line or figure that you grow out of. Likewise, the end of a line can be tucked back into the texture by combining it with the beginning of the next vocal phrase or connecting to the beginning of the next accompaniment figure or bass line.

Vary your accompaniment styles and, when playing fills behind the soloist, make them predictable so they can be coped with in a musical fashion. When and if the soloist riffs or repeats any phrase, use your ear training and the information from Chapter 2 on block voicing to reinforce the vocal line.

Given time, you will develop a certain ESP with your singer which will aid in the communication of starting pitches, ritards, length of fermatas, fluctuation of dynamics and all the nuances of a great performance. A fragment of a phrase thrown into a solo or a fill can propose or dictate the next tune in the set. Duke Ellington had numerous cues like this, such as little phrases he would play to let the band know it was time for intermission (intermission riffs).

Try to incorporate some or all of these ideas as you play the following blues with your favorite singer. Play it in all keys by yourself, then experiment with transpositions in rehearsal. There's a phrase provided at the end to show how you might bring it around to the top again for an additional verse or verses.

Duke Ellington (on right) and **Count Bas**
cornerstones of American jazz music. They f
brilliant big bands in the 1940s, '50s anc
Both were pianists of considerable skill with c
grounding in the

THE PERFECT BLUES

Track 29

= 120

If you want to write___ the per-fect blues,___

L.H. *8va* throughout

just speak from the heart so you won't con-fuse,___

and get in touch___ with your own___

___ sweet muse,___ to write___ the per-fect blues.___

CHAPTER 7

Chicago/Delta Blues

The massive migration of Southern Blacks to the north, beginning with World War I and continuing through the early 1970s, brought the Delta blues to urban centers, most notably Chicago. This transplanted blues had already changed considerably when Muddy Waters arrived in Chicago in 1943, and would change even more as Waters and others amplified their instruments to compete with noisy urban environments. Soon after arriving, Waters worked with piano players Memphis Slim and Sunnyland Slim. Later, he hired Otis Spann. Spann remained Waters' pianist for most of his career. Some other noted Chicago Blues pianists were Big Maceo (who worked with Tampa Red, replacing Tom Dorsey) and Little Brother Montgomery.

This new urban blues was influenced by jazz and later by Motown soul. Bass lines became more independent and prominent, horn sections were added and the presentation became more polished—sometimes even including uniforms and dance steps. Rather than being based on a repeated guitar or left-hand piano figure, a blues was more likely to be based on a repeated riff or riff-like bass figure. Jazz-style solos by horn players, guitar players and keyboardists began to be featured between vocal choruses. As a result of playing more with rhythm sections, piano players began using their left hands less. The minor blues scale became more prevalent, as did the shuffle feel with swung eighth notes. The music became more urgent and generally darker. Amplification allowed guitar players to draw Banshee shrieks out of bent strings which would have otherwise been barely audible. This, too, changed the style of playing. The old down-home styles were still used, but less frequently and recast in this more modern style. Different rural strains were combined in new and unusual ways because of the widespread roots of the migration, and a freer spirit of experimentation resulted in interesting hybrids. New Orleans influences, Latin and jump blues played by the big bands all had an impact.

The normal size of a working band also changed. The typical Delta blues ensemble ranged from a single guitar player to a piano duo or trio with bass and/or guitar. There might also be a violinist or harmonica player. Muddy Waters' band with two (and sometimes three) guitars, harmonica, piano, bass and drums became the model for all Chicago blues bands. The role of the piano player changed from providing fills and a foundation in the left hand to playing fills in free exchanges with the vocalist and the other musicians in the band.

The classic Chicago blues fill is an ascending segment of the blues scale, a repeated note, tremolo diad, tremolo octave or repeated scale segment, then a descending blues scale release. The starting point in the scale, length of scale and number of repetitions of the arrival point are all variable. The repetitions almost always reinforce the triplet-eighth pulse, although occasionally a player may play sixteenth notes or quarter-note triplets for a change of feel. Typically, while one player sounds the repeated notes or ostinato in the middle of the phrase, the other musicians will superimpose their own phrases of shorter length. The resulting structure becomes: vocal phrase; primary fill; subsidiary fills inside the primary fill; end of the primary fill.

Chicago Blues Fills

Measure:	1	2	3	4	5	6
Solo Phrase	VOCAL				VOCAL	
Primary fill						
Subsidiary fill						

Measure:	7	8	9	10	11	12
Solo Phrase			VOCAL		Turnaround..........................	
Primary fill						
Subsidiary fill						

The roles are not rigid and the overall texture is very *contrapuntal* (more than one melody at a time). Usually, no one really plays chords. However, someone is almost always sustaining a note or a tremolo so that the effect isn't too thin. If the vocal phrase is *compound* (built from sub-phrases) fills are inserted between the sub-phrases, often split between two different instruments.

James P. Johnson became known as the father of stride piano. In the 1920s his popularity flourished. He wrote many piano pieces, songs and Broadway shows.

PHOTO • COURTESY OF INSTITUTE OF JAZZ STUDIES

In this section, everything should be played with a swing feel unless marked "*Straight 8ths.*"

The recommended tempo for all the examples on this page is ♩ = 120.

The following examples typify how bass figures were transformed. Here is a familiar bass figure:

In Chicago style, this common shuffle bass line is played without *double stops* (two notes played simultaneously by one player).

Likewise, the *old-timey* two-beat of Delta blues....

...might become this:

or this:

The Motown influence is apparent in bass lines such as these:

Most endings in Chicago blues are variations on a final turnaround on the second half of the second beat of bar 12. Introductions are another story, forming almost a compendium of ways to start a blues.

With the expanded role of improvisation, an instrumental solo one chorus or more in length might precede the entrance of the singer. Partial choruses starting in bar 9 or bar 5 are also common, and the traditional half-cadence turnaround (ending on the V7 chord) also makes frequent appearances, usually decorated with improvisation. Sometimes, an open vamp on the I chord is used and, if the blues is based on a riff, a few repetitions of the riff make an adequate intro. Also not uncommon is starting with no introduction. At the other extreme, a *cadenza* (an unaccompanied solo passage) before the rest of the band enters is sometimes used—from a few pick-up notes in length to an entire verse. This first chorus is sometimes played *stop time*. In stop time, punctuations of the tonic chord or statements of a riff separate the vocal or instrumental phrases starting in bar 5, bar 9 or at the turnaround.

Punctuating the Tonic in Stop Time

Use of a Riff in Stop Time

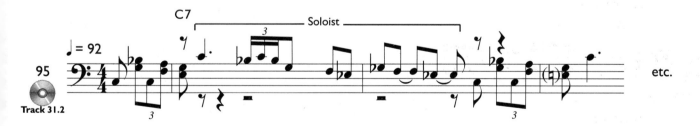

Below is a piece in the style of Otis Spann. Except where indicated (by the "L.H." marking), the left hand can play chord voicings in the comping register as a jazz pianist would.

Play along with the CD, leaving the bass line to the bass player or better yet, find yourself a bass player (a good bass figure shown at the end of the piece).

WORKIN' THE HAND SPANN BLUES

Here is the suggested bass figure for this tune.

The playing of Eurreal "Little Brother" Montgomery was influenced by jazz. He led a swing band in the 1930s in Mississippi but became a fixture of the Chicago blues scene. This piano solo incorporates some of the elements of his style.

Track 33

YOUR BROTHER'S KEEPER BLUES

CHAPTER 8

New Orleans R&B

MUSICAL GUMBO

In this section, everything should be played with a swing feel unless marked *"Straight 8ths."*

New Orleans, renowned as the birthplace of jazz, was the intersection of five major cultures: African, French, Spanish, Celtic and American Indian. Traces of these influences are apparent in New Orleans blues.

New Orleans R&B shares with jazz the African features of call and response, African rhythms and the blues scale used over European harmonies (first fused in the spiritual Protestant hymns sung in an African style—probably beginning in the earliest days of slavery). Unlike Chicago-style blues, the major forms of the blues scale predominate in New Orleans blues.

The French and Spanish influences are apparent in the preference for eight-bar blues and thirty-two-bar song form in New Orleans blues. This is a remnant of the dance music which the Europeans brought with them. The biggest influence, however, comes through the *Contredanse,* in particular the *Cinque,* an Africanization of a European dance form with a five-note rhythm:

A

Track 34.1

B

The so called *second line,* almost always present in New Orleans music, is the *clavé* rhythm. To the present day, rock'n'roll and R&B are still underpinned by the clave.

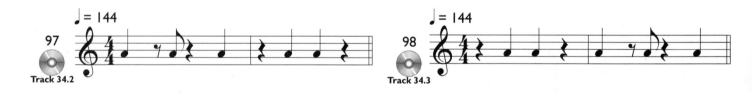

Track 34.2   Track 34.3

Like gumbo, a New Orleans dish that contains a little bit of everything at hand, music in New Orleans is a mixture of ragtime, Dixieland jazz, Cajun (French Acadian), Zydeco, rhumba, mambo, Calypso, flamenco, Celtic jigs and reels and Irish ballads.

New Orleans blues reflects its proximity to and shared history with all these styles.

LONGHAIR BLUES

In the *Intermediate* section, you were introduced to the reputation and musical style of Roy Byrd, A.K.A Professor Longhair. Two of his influences were Sullivan Rock and Robert Bertrand ("Kid Stormy Weather"), and he is regarded as a forefather of Mac Rebennack ("Dr. John"), Allan Toussaint, James Booker, Huey "Piano" Smith, Fats Domino, Harry Connick, Jr. and many others. Collecting and studying recordings of these artists is highly recommended.

Right-hand figures in the New Orleans piano style tend towards a high degree of ornamentation and much use of repeated short figures. These are both melodic groove figures designed to propel the feel and the time. One of Professor Longhair's pet phrases is an arpeggio or pentatonic scale, usually descending, with a single sixteenth-note triplet turn.

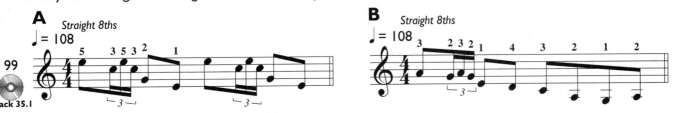

Figures with double stops moving in parallel motion and chromatic passing tones in the lower voice are common.

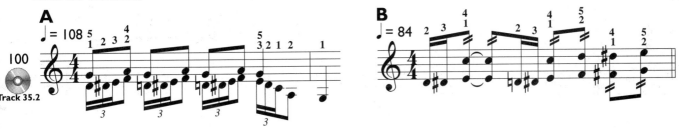

Tremolos are common, but more often as the beginnings or ends of phrases, unlike Chicago blues where they appear more frequently at the peaks.

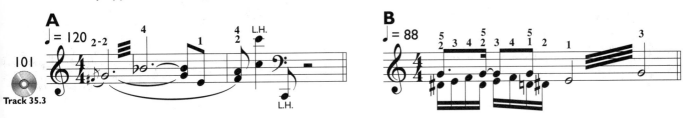

Humorous, quotation-like interjections seeming to come from completely different styles and unrelated tunes are a favorite device. This is another reflection on the musical diversity of the region.

Since the emphasis is on feel rather than on virtuosity, right-hand figures that merely outline the harmony or divide the chord into two parts, creating a cross-rhythmic pulse, are abundant.

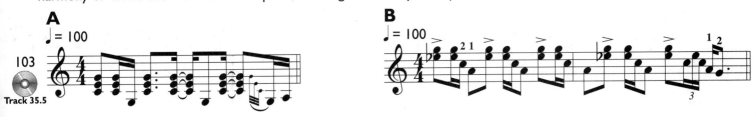

NEW ORLEANS ACCOMPANIMENT STYLES

A typical New Orleans tune is as recognizable by its feel and accompaniment as it is by its melodic and lyrical content. Below is a list of just a few possibilities. You will have to augment this list through your continued listening studies.

1. The always-present dotted-quarter note bass line (the three-note part of the clavé), with its myriad variations, straight or swung, with the right hand playing eighth notes, quarter notes or any number of groove figures.

2. The walking bass in quarter notes (in the boogie-woogie style, not a free walking line). This can be straight or swung, with right-hand chords on the off-beats. (The bass line often has broken octaves, since that is a similar effect to playing chords on the off-beats.)

3. Decoration of the clave in the right hand over a walking bass (repeated figure) or divided between the two hands.

4. Stride, in its pure form, makes many appearances. It also appears with the backbeat doubled in a swing eighth feel, reflecting a West Indian influence.

---

5. In Chapter 4, we introduced the concept of bass notes alternating with chords in a rudimental pattern in the style of James Booker. This also occurs in quarter notes as an alternative to stride.

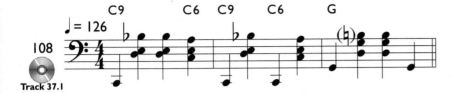

6. Another James Booker favorite is this one bar repeated left-hand rhythm.

7. Shuffle-type bass lines, of a type borrowed from Chicago blues, are sometimes used as are some classic boogie-woogie broken-octave figures.

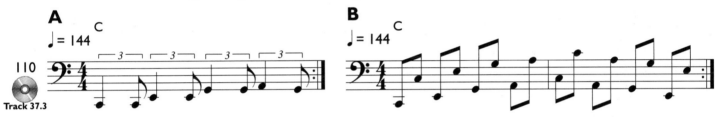

8. The clavé rhythm is sometimes played as a double-time riff over either a walking line or the dotted-quarter rhythm variations.

9. Many bass lines are borrowed from R&B and 1950s rock 'n' roll:

When looking for recordings of Alan Toussaint, called by some "The Bach of New Orleans," you will find some early recordings under the name *Tousan*. The following piece is in the style of those early recordings, which already exhibit the clarity of form and virtuosic simplicity that are featured in his work as a major producer of R&B.

Track 38

ODE: TOUSAN—ITY BLUES

D.S. al Coda

James Booker was probably the New Orleans pianist most respected by his peers. Booker was a musical genius of the first order. Classically trained, he played Chopin from memory at a very early age, and it is said he could play solos that he heard for the first time *backwards*. This title comes from something he was quoted as saying while sailing near the end of his life.

JAMMIN' WITH THE WIND

Track 39

CHAPTER 9

Burnin', Layin' Back and Bringin' It All Home

By now you know that rhythmic content in the blues is paramount. Mainstream artists stay very close to a handful of chord progressions, a few scales, even fewer meters and the subject matter of the lyrics stays within fairly narrow confines. Every tune will have one or two fresh devices used to distinguish it from others, but the real creative energy is expended inventing a unique rhythmic feel and using signature or spontaneously composed rhythmic devices in solos.

To use a single rhythmic value through an entire solo, possible, would be not be in the style. It would not e the listener as intensely as moving from one rhythmic to another. Think of the available rhythmic values, from smallest subdivision to the longest note you can con of playing. Now make a list of these rhythmic values, sixteenth-note triplets or thirty-second notes as the fa to tied whole notes. Think of this list as being your "s of rhythmic values.

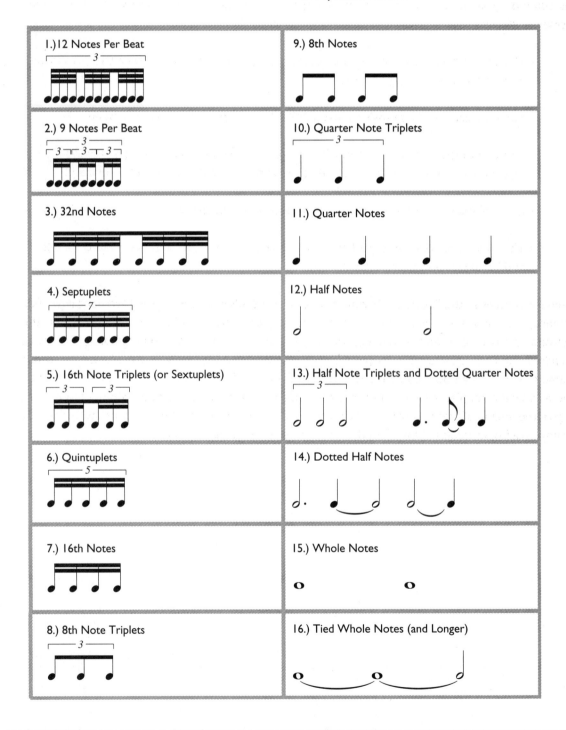

Each of the rhythmic values has a feel that is affected by the pulse of the meter in the rhythm section underneath it. If the rhythm in your solo makes a polyrhythm (page 245) when paired with the meter of the rhythm section, the result is a gain of energy and interest. This is because the two rhythms will make a larger number of attacks in different places within the bar and because of the division of the listener's attention between the two rhythmic streams.

One often-used rhythmic contour is moving from smaller subdivisions (the low end of our "scale") to larger values in mid-phrase and back at phrase end. The effect of this is an increase in emotional tension followed by a release. If the longer notes are tremolos, one might consider this to be movement from slightly larger values to the smaller values in the tremolo or trill.

The opposite shape is also typical—moving from large note values to faster movement in the phrase giving an effect called *burning* or *wailing* mid-flight.

It is common practice to use smaller subdivisions at phrase beginnings and endings. This results in several effects:

- The soloist seems to have an inexhaustible supply of ideas and is trying to get as many as possible out in a single breath.

- The interest level is intensified just before the next breath or pause is taken.

- The end of the phrase seems much less final, and the motion is better sustained from one phrase to the next because the actual end point is more difficult to discern.

- Every phrase has greater tension at the center, less at the ends.

- The illusion of *riding* on top of the rhythm section is enhanced by seeming to tumble and having to regain one's equilibrium.

Some movement in the "Scale of Rhythmic Values" is a traditional part of the blues language. For instance, beginning a line with an ascending scale in quarter-note triplets, usually leaving out the first one or more notes and continuing with either faster or slower movement, is associated with *soulfulness*, and the quarter-note triplets call attention to the beginning of the phrase. Another example would be an *ostinato* figure (a repeated figure) in faster values as the peak of a phrase. And as a final example, the tried-and-true tactic of beginning with large note values, played so as to give the feeling of mass, moving gradually to smaller note values as the solo progresses for that speedy, macho, muscular, "leave 'em drenched in their own sweat" climax.

To get the full effect of a slow blues, motion on the "Scale of Rhythmic Values" must be downward, from smaller to larger note values, usually between adjacent levels. The line being played this way must have a logical and predictable sense of motion. The predictability of the line is what allows the soloist to pull the audience onto a separate rhythmic plane, slower than that of the rhythm section. This can be done by simply slowing the end of a phrase so it's extended past the bar line.

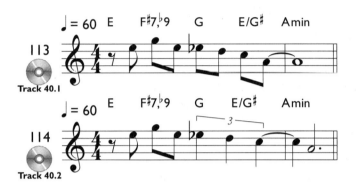

In this section, everything should be played with a swing feel unless marked "Straight 8ths."

Or, totally disregard the band's tempo and grind to a halt at the end of a solo.

Extremely slow blues tempos represent a plane of reality far removed from the tempo of modern life. The soloist who can ride the feel comfortably and bring the listener into that plane is a master of the art of the blues.

PHOTO • COURTESY OF INSTITUTE OF JAZZ STUDIES

Roosevelt "The Honeydripper" Sykes, born in 1906, was equally gifted as a blues pianist, songwriter and singer. He frequently sang while he played, but also accompanied many great blues vocalists. Roosevelt began his career in St. Louis at the age of 14, ran away to play in barrelhouses in Mississippi and Louisiana when he was 15, and made his first recording for Okeh records in New York at the age of 23. He later spent a great deal of time in Chicago where he was an integral part of the Chicago blues scene, influencing many young pianists, especially Memphis Slim. Listen to blues by Roosevelt "The Honeydripper" Sykes on Smithsonian/Folkways recordings for some incredible playing.

A further use for slowing over the time—moving sequentially downward in our "Scale of Rhythmic Values"—is to signal that the end of your solo or the tune is near. These cues can be quite subtle or obvious, reversing the process discussed in the *Burnin'* section. That is to say, the fast movement of solos and melody can give way to increasingly slower note values. This creates the illusion that the quick, seemingly easy movement in the flight of the tune had so much momentum that it required industrial strength muscle to stop it. Simply playing a cliché turnaround after a long solo is a perfect way to stop this momentum and, along with plain old shoe familiarity, at least part of the reason the traditional final cadence is so satisfying.

Another way of delaying the end of the tune is the *tag*. A basic blues tag is done by remaining on the tonic in bars 11 and 12, and then returning to bar 9 to repeat the final four bars, thus increasing the importance and inevitability of the final turnaround. If you are playing in a band, this may have to be worked out in advance.

If you are using ii7 and V7 in bars 9 and 10, a further possibility is the *"really mean it"* ending. This is a deceptive cadence to the iii7 chord (or III7, making it a *secondary dominant*—dominant of the VI). Or, you can play a deceptive cadence to the ♭VII7, the tritone substitute for III7. In either case, you then play a cycle of 5ths back to the tonic (ii-V-I). In a more jazz-oriented context, ♭iii7 and ♭VI7 can be substituted for iii7 and VI7.

Choose any one of these three…

Measure:	9	10	11	12
Possible Harmonies:	V7	IV7	I	I
	ii7	V7	III7 or ♭VII7	VI7
	ii7	V7	♭iii7	♭VI7

…followed by a tag:

Measure:	9	10	11		12	
Possible Harmonies:	V7	IV7	I	IV	I V7	I
	ii7	V7	I	IV	I V7	I

One sometimes hears the III7 – VII7 – ii7 –V7 section of the progression repeated three times. Occasionally, as Claire Fischer, the West Coast keyboard master and composer once said, it can become "… one of those tunes where the coda goes on to become a separate tune."

In this piano solo, which uses some of the ideas we just introduced, your mission—should you accept it—is to write your own melody over this left-hand figure. Use the melody provided here as inspiration. Play the second chorus over this bass line. Remember, there are twelve eighth notes in the bar.

If you are playing along with the CD, take a so during the repeat of th A section.

BLUES FOR HEAVY ROTATION

CHAPTER 10

Boogie-Woogie

When the barrelhouse pianists of the logging camps in the Southern United States followed the northward migration, their music morphed into a more sophisticated, urban music which came to be known as boogie-woogie. You have already been introduced to Jimmy Yancey and Clarence "Pine Top" Smith. Some other names associated with the style are Pete Johnson, Albert Ammons, Cow Cow Davenport, Hershal Thomas and Meade "Lux" Lewis.

Clarence Smith's *Pine Top Boogie* was the first major boogie-woogie hit in 1928, and Tommy Dorsey's version of the tune (1938) began the second wave of popularity which lasted through World War II, peaking with *Boogie-Woogie Bugle Boy* by the Andrews Sisters.

BASS LINES

The essential element in boogie-woogie is the left-hand bass ostinato (examples 116, 118-121) comprised of eight eighth notes (as codified by the pop hit, *Beat Me, Daddy, Eight to the Bar* by Will Bradley). Generally, some kind of double melodic line is present or implied. Broken octaves are often a feature, as well. Right-hand material is often rhythmic rather than melodic. When it is melodic, it is relatively simple and repetitive, designed to create cross rhythms and syncopations. Chord progressions in boogie-woogie are usually very basic, omitting the turnaround in bars 11 and 12, remaining on the I chord, and seldom using the IV chord in bar 2. In bars 9 and 10, iimin7 to V7 and V7 to IV7 are common, but of equal or greater frequency is remaining on the V chord through both bars.

> In this section, everything should be played with a swing feel unless marked *"Straight 8ths."*

Here is an abbreviated catalog of left- and right-hand boogie-woogie figures.

In the style of the left-hand part of *Honky Tonk Train Blues* by Meade "Lux" Lewis:

Also in the style of *Honky Tonk Train Blues*, this is an interesting example of the double melodic line in the right hand.

Both Albert Ammons and Meade "Lux" Lewis sometimes use a "block voice" bass line.

= Roll the chord.

Here is another left-hand figure in the style of Albert Ammons' *Boogie-Woogie Stomp*.

Here is a bass line in the style of Pete Johnson's *Roll Em' Pete*, also called *Climbin' and Screamin'*.

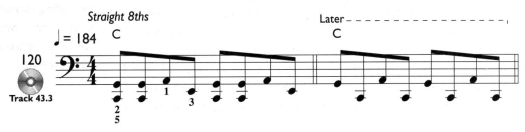

Here are two left-hand figures in the style of James P. Johnson.

Here is a challenge for you. Meade "Lux" Lewis recorded an amazing piece called *Variations on a Theme, Part I – 19 Ways of Playing a Chorus* (on harpsichord!). The chord progression is the simplest possible, using the V chord in bars 9 and 10 and the I chord in bars 11 and 12. Below is a list of nineteen motifs in the style of those he used to develop each chorus. See if you can create a chorus using each. After you have done this, compare your results with Lewis'. (The CD is "Blue Boogie, Boogie-woogie, Stride and the Piano Blues," on Bluenote CPD 7990992.)

BASS LINE:

MOTIFS:

This piece uses the boogie-woogie style combined with more contemporary jazz harmonies such as the ♯9. It uses a device called *octave displacement* —putting one note in a line an octave higher or lower, either in the left hand and/or the right hand. For instance, look at the bass line in the second half of bar 3. The A in the line F♯, G, A is displaced up one octave.

Track 44

THE STAR BOOGIE

CHAPTER 11

Gospel

BACKGROUND

As the channel for African musical influence in America, the Black church is the source of almost all our popular musical styles. From as early as 1750, there are reports of slaves singing Protestant hymns in a specialized way complete with descriptions of call and response in the form of *lining out* (chanting or singing a line sometimes using a different melody than the hymn being performed). This style of singing spread throughout the U.S. with the various "awakenings" and "revivals" of the late 1800s and early 1900s, taking root most strongly in the South. The Baptist, Methodist and Pentecostal churches all developed their own idiomatic strains, with the Pentecostal's being the most uninhibited expression, including percussion instruments, stamping, clapping and shouting. In the early 1900s, the Jubilee Quartet, which was four male voices singing a'capella, became the dominant Gospel performing group.

One of the first Gospel pianists and singers was Arizona Dranes. She set the classic Gospel accompaniment style with her combination of Protestant hymn harmony, ragtime two-beat and elements of barrelhouse piano. She was also one of the first to record that stylized triplet feel which, by the 1950s, had become the familiar $\frac{12}{8}$.

In Chapter 7, you were introduced to Thomas A. Dorsey who, with Hudson Whittaker (Tampa Red), had several non-religious chart hits. After a nervous break-down, Dorsey returned to Gospel music. Previously he had lived a "double life." Even his parents didn't know of his career playing "the Devil's music." He became known as the father of Gospel music.

Another sacred keyboardist who had a career in secular music was Kenneth Morris, who first used the Hammond organ in Gospel music. The piano and Hammond together are considered the perfect accompaniment in Gospel circles. Both Dorsey and Morris were prolific composers and became important publishers in the Gospel field as well.

Some other early pianists and organists who deserve mention are:

Estelle Allen
Mildred Falls
Evelyn Gay
Gwendolyn Cooper Lightener

All four of these artists were pianists for Mahalia Jackson, the New Orleans-based gospel singer, at one time or another. Jackson was a strictly spiritual singer (she would not perform in clubs) and was world famous until her death in 1972. Her first hit was *Lift Every Voice And Sing* in 1956. She recorded with Duke Ellington, sang for presidents and performed at many of Martin Luther King's appearances.

In the 1950s, pianists were so integral to the music that their names were often included in the group's name. Some important players of this time were:

Curtis Dublin, whose style incorporated elements of jazz.

Herbert Pickard

Roberta Martin, who was the pianist for Thomas Dorsey's Gospel choir at the Pilgrim Baptist Church and later, an important exponent of Gospel music with her group, the Roberta Martin Singers.

Clara Ward of the Clara Ward Singers.

The third wave of Gospel keyboardists includes such artists as:

Doris Akers, a composer, director and arranger who started as a singer in the *Sally Martin Singers*. Martin was an associate of Thomas Dorsey.

"Professor" Alex Bradford

James Cleveland, a composer and arranger of prodigious ability who directed and coached many prominent Gospel groups and was an architect of the modern Gospel sound.

Jessy Dixon

James Herndon

Raymond Rasberry

Lawrence Roberts

Charles Taylor

Gospel music has always been an enormous influence on jazz artists (such as Cannonball Adderly, Oliver Nelson, Joseph Zawinul and Charles Mingus) and R&B musicians (not just Sam Cooke, Al Green and others who started in Gospel, but practically every Motown artist). Gospel music entered the Pop realm with the Edwin Hawkins crossover hit of 1969, *O Happy Day*. Many genres have been adapted for use in Gospel music, from Handel's *Messiah* (Quincy Jones) to the most current pop and R&B stylings. It has also been a tradition to write religious words to popular songs.

In this book we will touch only on the basics of "classic" Gospel. For further guidance, the prescription is a heavy dose of listening to the recordings of all the artists listed here, watching or listening to Gospel shows and/or attendance at the Pentecostal church of your choice.

The first element in Gospel piano accompaniment is heavy repeated chords, usually with octave doublings in close position played in the comping register. If you have to go out of the comping register, extend it downward rather than upward. The chord is often broken into two parts and used as a groove figure, or the IV chord is inserted in the middle of the rhythmic figure for added motion. Note that gospel tunes are frequently in $\frac{3}{4}$.

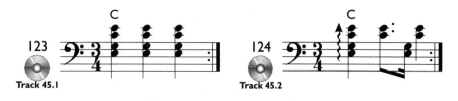

123 Track 45.1

124 Track 45.2

In this section, everything should be played with a swing feel unless marked "*Straight 8ths*."

125 Track 45.3

The recommended tempo for all the examples on this page is ♩ = 84.

The second element is the bass line in octaves, usually in the lowest possible register for weight, with diatonic or chromatic sweeps leading into each new chord root.

126 Track 45.4

The third element is fills, which can be in the bass register as well as the treble, and are often in octaves, although single-note runs are also frequent. These runs usually have just a handful of notes. Pentatonic rather than diatonic scales prevail.

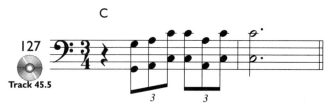

127 Track 45.5

128 Track 45.6

Cadences are typically *plagal* (I – IV – I) or iimin7 – V7 with the bass line harmonized (iimin7 – iiimin7 – IV — ♯ivdim – V).

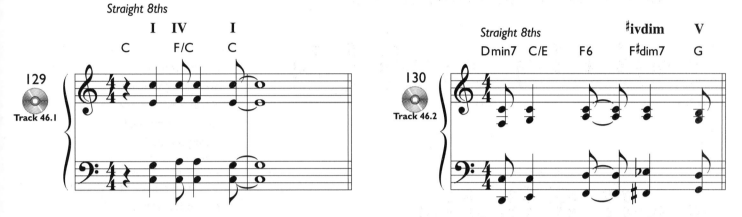

Another common harmonic structure borrowed from European music via the Protestant hymnal is I – iimin7 – I – IV   or   IV – I– iimin7 – I.

The vamp, built on a repeated phrase in the chorus (usually just two chords to facilitate improvisation, although sometimes more) shows up in a high percentage of Gospel compositions. This is the place where vocalists exhibit their highest degree of artistry and where choir and congregation are in the heights of religious fervor. The vamp may be longer than the rest of the tune several times over. The close of the vamp is often signaled by some variation of the choral phrase or a preset phrase from the soloist. Endings often include virtuoso cadenza displays from the soloist, and, if audience enthusiasm warrants, some portion of the vamp and the final cadence are likely to be reprised.

CHAPTER 12

Jazz and Fusion Blues

All serious jazz players acknowledge the importance of the blues and most consider themselves to be blues players. However, when saying they "play the blues," they mean they use the twelve-bar blues form with sophisticated changes, usually in the key of F, as a framework for virtuosic improvisation. The vocabulary of the blues is present in the playing of a high percentage of jazz artists and serves as a counterbalance against a level of complexity that would lose touch with the average listener, a tendency that is recurrent in jazz. In this method, we have already mentioned many pianists who had credible reputations as both jazz and blues pianists.

Twentieth-century jazz can be roughly divided into four chronological styles/eras using major artists as references:

1. **Traditional Jazz** (Ragtime, Dixieland through Big Band Swing): Scott Joplin, Edward Kennedy "Duke" Ellington, William "Count" Basie and a host of other big band pianists, along with Fats Waller, Jelly Roll Morton, Art Tatum, Oscar Peterson and their peers.

2. **Bop and Post Bop**: Charlie Parker, Dizzy Gillespie, Charles Mingus; pianists Bud Powell, Thelonius Monk, Lenny Tristano, Tommy Flanagan, McCoy Tyner and others too numerous to mention.

3. **Cool and Modal Jazz**: Miles Davis in his middle years, pianists Bill Evans, Horace Silver, Red Garland, Wynton Kelly, Herbie Hancock … the list goes on.

4. **Jazz Rock/Fusion**: Miles Davis again, post "Bitches Brew" and "Live Evil" with keyboard players Herbie Hancock (again—a major figure), Keith Jarrett, Joseph Zawinul, Chick Corea and a host of others.

The popularity of traditional jazz continues to the present day, as does that of hard bop. Post bop, as typified by John Coltrane, branched off into free jazz—the so called "New Thing"—in the early and middle 1960s. This was "reaction music" utilizing the skills of the bop school. The influence of the modal period is still evident in "smooth jazz" and the atmospheric waftings of New Age mood music. However, smooth jazz is actually the disowned step-child of the fusion movement, and fusion itself has been disowned by many proponents of the other styles.

What all these different styles share, and what distinguishes them from mainstream blues, is the playing of changes—finding an appropriate scale for each chord (whatever its duration). In mainstream blues, we usually play from a parent scale (usually some form of the blues scale) over a group of related chord changes. In this chapter, we'll take a look at information and concepts that go along with playing changes.

NATURAL MODES AND SYNTHETIC SCALES

The first place to look for a scale to fit a given chord is the twelve major key signatures, each of which contains seven natural modes. The modes are listed below with the Greek names customarily assigned to them and the chords (with all extensions), that they can be used over.

IONIAN (SAME AS THE MAJOR SCALE)

(or 9, or 13)
C Maj7

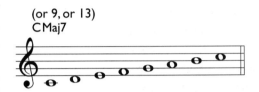

DORIAN

(or 9, or 11, or 13)
D min7

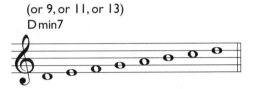

PHRYGIAN

(or 11)
E min7

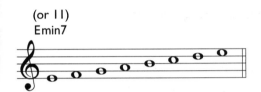

LYDIAN

(or 9, or +11, or 13)
F Maj7

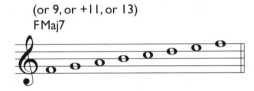

MIXOLYDIAN

(or 11)
B min7♭5

AEOLIAN (SAME AS THE NATURAL MINOR SCALE)

(or 9, or 11)
A min7

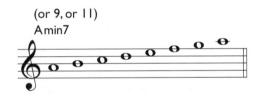

LOCRIAN

(or F/G)
(or 9, or 13)
G7

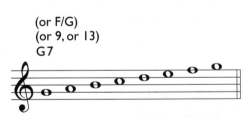

Play each scale over the 7th chord indicated in all keys. As you do this, see if you can feel the resolution tendency of each half step. Each mode has its own unique flavor and extra-musical associations. Ionian and Aeolian are the familiar major and minor, Dorian is characterized as "heroic," although it has associations with Celtic folk melodies as well. Phrygian clearly says "Spanish." Lydian is generally delicate and otherworldly, while Mixolydian, with its flatted 7th degree, has an earthy connection to the blues. The Locrian mode is infrequently used in a modal way. Rather, it is more often found in the context of a chord progression. It suggests the grotesque and misshapen. Become familiar with them all!

Make sure that you are fluent with the modes in all keys. This is not terribly difficult—if you have a secure knowledge of key signatures, and memorize which degree of the major scale is the root of each mode, it is not a great leap to play in any chosen mode in any key. Try all the modes shown above in all keys. You should also determine the whole-step/half-step structure of each mode and memorize them. For example, practice playing all seven modes from the same root (C Ionian, C Dorian, C Phrygian, etc.).

PLAYING CHANGES

Having established the scale for each chord in a given chord progression, the next step in learning to improvise in a jazz style is to practice running motifs through the changes. Here is an example of a simple motif over a turnaround:

Begin to collect motifs for jazz playing. You will need many. Keep them in your notebook. Remember the "Golden Rule of Repetition" (see page 211): do not use a single pattern more than three times without alteration, except when practicing.

EXTENSIONS AND ALTERED EXTENSIONS

Jazz differs from blues in that more extended harmonies are used. When voicing extensions in the left hand, the 9th can replace the root and the 11th and/or 13th can replace the 5th. Altering the extension can heighten the tension this creates—9ths can be sharped or flatted, 11ths can be augmented and 13ths flatted (a flatted 13th implies that a 5th is present in the chord, otherwise it would sound the same as an augmented 5th). Example 134 shows some common extended chords as they would be voiced in the right hand, without roots or 5ths.

Scales must be altered to fit these altered extensions. Here, the F is sharped to conform to the altered 11th.

In this example, the D and A are flatted to conform to the altered 9th and 13th, respectively.

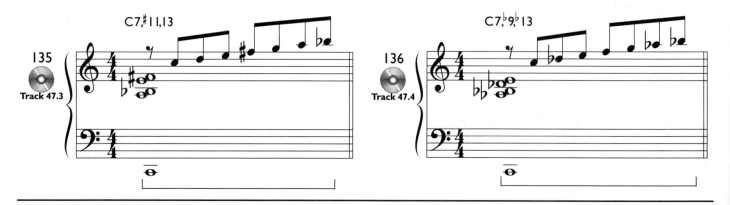

These two choruses use a handful of motifs in a mainstream-jazz style. They illustrate playing the changes. Notice how a passage in the blues scale (the last two bars) brings the solo back down to earth. Keep the left hand simple so that you can focus on how the lines work with the harmonies.

Track 48

THE BLUES CHANGES EVERYTHING

Beginning in the 1960s, jazz was radically transformed by the fusion movement. The "third stream" experiments of the 1950s, combining jazz with European classical music, were followed by experiments with Indian classical music, Arabic, Balinese, Japanese, Celtic, traditional African music from all parts of that continent and the contemporary European "avante garde." "World music" collaborations and unusual instrumentations thrived. People like Dave Brubeck, Don Ellis, Miles Davis and John McLaughlin's Mahavishnu Orchestra played the blues in odd meters. The use of space, pioneered by Basie and Monk, became cosmic in the recordings of Miles Davis. There were experiments with playing in two simultaneous meters. Indian rhythmic structures and scales and European *twelve-tone rows* (a modern classical compositional technique) occasionally found their way into blues compositions. The harmonic vocabulary, already having adopted the harmonic innovations of the French impressionists (chord extensions), expanded to include other techniques such as *polytonality* (playing in more than one key simultaneously). Players sometimes superimposed melodies or improvised lines with new key centers over the blues progression, and borrowings were made from the more extreme harmonic and formal experimentation of Igor Stravinsky, Bela Bartok, Edgar Varese, Olivier Messiaen and Karlheinz Stockhausen.

A telling example of the limits to which the blues have stretched is *Celestial Terrestrial Commuters* on *The Mahav* Orchestra's "Birds of Fire" LP. The band members impro freely over an eleven-bar form in $\frac{19}{16}$ ($\frac{6}{8} + \frac{6}{16}$ separated by a s sixteenth note.) The subdominant is replaced by the II c in bar 4 and by the $^\flat$iii chord in bar 9. The dominant is rep by the $^\flat$V chord. The scale of the ostinato which the tune is on is transposed to each of these scale degrees. It is a n scale with a raised 4th degree and a lowered 7th degree. melody uses this scale, also, but mixes in substantial ma from the familiar blues scale. The soloists all regroup subdivisions within each bar and always come out on downbeat. All this at the rapid pace of over 400 sixte notes per minute! This was a stunning display of musicia and compositional skill from an unearthly realm, yet it i easily recognizable as the blues.

In the following composition you may be able to identify of these devices. Notice that each measure of 22 eighth r is divided into three sub-measures ($\frac{5}{4}$, $\frac{6}{8}$ and $\frac{6}{8}$) marked dotted bar lines. Count "1 & 2 & 3 & 4 & 5 &, 1 2 3 4 1 2 3 4 5 6" keeping the speed of the eighth notes st Have fun!

GLOBAL VILLAGE BLUES

Track 49

INTO THE FUTURE

Congratulations on having completed *The Complete Blues Keyboard Method.*

Traditionally, becoming a blues player meant becoming a sideman with an established artist for a number of years. If such an opportunity presents itself, jump on it! In the meantime, play every chance you get with players better than yourself to improve your skills. Teach players less proficient than you are, not only to solidify your own understanding and performance but also to continue, on some level, the verbal transmission of knowledge which is traditional in the blues.

Until recent years, the bandstand was the only blues school. Recording technology breakthroughs, specifically CD players that can advance through a tune one note at a time and also slow a tune without changing its pitch, have made transcription and rote memorization possible—even for musicians with only modest ear training. There are also numerous published collections of keyboard solos from prominent artists. The technology and methods such as this however, cannot completely replace the mentor/apprentice relationship.

At the very least, it is hoped this method has given you a glimpse into the vastness of the blues and given you an appreciation for the geniuses who originated and developed the music. It is also hoped that you have gained a sense of certainty that the blues will endure. Whatever devices we may use to make our music, the unbroken thread of the blues will always be there to remind us of who we are and where we have been; it will continue to humanize our music and our lives.

DISCOGRAPHY

Atlantic Blues	Four-CD set including blues piano compilation with Jimmy Yancey, Professor Longhair, Meade Lux Lewis, etc. There is also great piano playing on the vocal and guitar compilations. (Atlantic Records)
Blues by Roosevelt Sykes	Roosevelt Sykes. (Smithsonian Folkways)
Blues Essentials	Compilation with Muddy Waters, Elmore James, Memphis Slim, Howlin Wolf, etc. (Capitol Records)
Birth of Soul	Ray Charles. (Atlantic Records)
Boogie Woogie, Stride and Piano Blues	With Pete Johnson, James P. Johnson, etc. (EMI Records)
Dr. John Plays Mac Rebbenack	Dr. John. (Rounder Records) Solo piano. (Clean Cuts Records)
Essential Blues Piano	Great blues piano compilation with Otis Spann, Lafayette Leake, Pinetop Perkins, Katie Webster, etc. (House of Blues)
Hoochie Coochie Man/ Got My Mojo Workin'	Jimmy Smith. (Verve Records)
Jump Back Honey	Hadda Brooks. The complete Okeh sessions. (Columbia)
Live and Well Live at the Regal	B.B. King. (MCA Records)
New Orleans Piano	Professor Longhair. (Atlantic)
Memphis Slim	Memphis Slim. (Chess MCA Records)
Patriarch of the Blues	Sunnyland Slim. (Opal Records)
Rekooperation	Al Kooper. (BMG Music)
Spiders on the Keys	James Booker. (Rounder)
Texas Flood	Stevie Ray Vaughan. (Epic records). Classic example of modern blues guitar.
The Blues Never Die	Otis Spann. (Prestige Records)
The Chess 50th Anniversary Collection	Muddy Waters. (Chess/MCA Records)
The Complete Recordings	Robert Johnson. No keyboards here, but he may be the most important blues artist ever. (Columbia Records)
Vocal Accompaniment and Early Post-war Recordings: 1930-1954	Little Brother Montgomery. (Document Records)